AMERICAN

HERITAGE

April 1958 · Volume IX, Number 3

"RUNAWAY HORSE"

This painting, executed about 1850 by an unknown artist, typifies a vigorous new departure in nineteenth-century American art. As the colonial period ended, our artists ceased to copy European styles and developed their own—crude and naïve by Continental standards, but stamped with the freshness and strength of a genuine folk art. Much of the work of the period was done by itinerant painters who earned their bread and butter painting houses, barns, or tavern signs, and many canvases showed it. But some, like Runaway Horse, *were sophisticated in style and almost mystical in mood. In* Paintings from America *John Walker suggests that for this artist at least "animals, like the free-running horse and the dog at his heels, represent the beauty and poetry of nature running away from the civilization of the little human bystanders."*

AMERICAN HERITAGE

The Magazine of History

PUBLISHER
James Parton

EDITORIAL DIRECTOR
Joseph J. Thorndike, Jr.

EDITOR
Bruce Catton

MANAGING EDITOR
Oliver Jensen

ASSOCIATE EDITORS
Richard M. Ketchum
Joan Paterson Mills

ASSISTANT EDITOR
Robert L. Reynolds

EDITORIAL ASSISTANTS
Hilde Heun, Stephen W. Sears
Caroline Backlund, Lilyan Goldman
Helen M. Brown, Robert Cowley
Art: **Murray Belsky, Trudy Glucksberg**

ART DIRECTOR
Irwin Glusker

ADVISORY BOARD
Allan Nevins, *Chairman*
Carl Carmer   Richard P. McCormick
Albert B. Corey   Harry Shaw Newman
Christopher Crittenden   Howard H. Peckham
Marshall B. Davidson   S. K. Stevens
Louis C. Jones   Arthur M. Schlesinger, Sr.

REGIONAL EDITORS
Ray A. Billington . . . .*Evanston, Illinois*
John W. Caughey. . . .*Los Angeles, California*
K. Ross Toole . . . .*Helena, Montana*
Walter Prescott Webb . . . .*Austin, Texas*

STAFF PHOTOGRAPHER
Herbert Loebel

CIRCULATION DIRECTOR
Richard V. Benson

AMERICAN HERITAGE is published every two
months by American Heritage Publishing Co.,
Inc., 551 Fifth Avenue, New York 17, N. Y.

Single Copies: $2.95
Annual Subscriptions: $12.50 in the U.S.A.
$13.50 elsewhere

An annual Index of AMERICAN HERITAGE is
published every February, priced at $1.00.
AMERICAN HERITAGE is also indexed in
Readers' Guide to Periodical Literature.

AMERICAN HERITAGE will consider but assumes
no responsibility for unsolicited material.

Sponsored by

American Association for State & Local History • Society of American Historians

CONTENTS   *April, 1958 · Volume IX, Number 3*

COVER: A little over a century ago the appearance off the Japanese coast of Commodore Matthew Calbraith Perry and a United States Navy squadron shocked the Japanese people and stirred their empire out of its stultifying isolation. (An article on this subject begins on page 12.) This rice-paper drawing of Perry and his principal aide, Captain Henry A. Adams, was one of scores made by eager, curious Japanese artists. It is published through the kindness of the Commodore's great-great-grandnephew, the Reverend DeWolf Perry of Charleston, South Carolina. *On the back cover:* The illustration of a soulful-eyed boy and his best friend, an equally soulful-eyed Saint Bernard, is from an 1860 song sheet cover in the collection of Lester S. Levy of Baltimore *(see page 52).*

HOW THE FRONTIER SHAPED THE AMERICAN CHARACTER

By RAY ALLEN BILLINGTON

Since the dawn days of historical writing in the United States, historians have labored mightily, and usually in vain, to answer the famous question posed by Hector St. John de Crèvecœur in the eighteenth century: "What then is the American, this new man?" Was that composite figure actually a "new man" with unique traits that distinguished him from his Old World ancestors? Or was he merely a transplanted European? The most widely accepted—and bitterly disputed—answer was advanced by a young Wisconsin historian named Frederick Jackson Turner in 1893. The American was a new man, he held, who owed his distinctive characteristics and institutions to the unusual New World environment—characterized by the availability of free land and an ever-receding frontier —in which his civilization had grown to maturity. This environmental theory, accepted for a generation after its enunciation, has been vigorously attacked and vehemently defended during the past two decades. How has it fared in this battle of words? Is it still a valid key to the meaning of American history?

Turner's own background provides a clue to the answer. Born in Portage, Wisconsin, in 1861 of pioneer

TEXT CONTINUED ON PAGE 7

"frontier theory" is still a valid key to understanding modern America

Although John Gast painted this canvas in 1872, twenty years before Turner's essay on the significance of the frontier, its theme might have sprung straight from the pages themselves. Here is Turner's procession of civilization—"the buffalo following the trail to the salt springs, the Indian, the fur-trader and hunter, the cattle raiser, the pioneer farmer."

Turner states his frontier theory: 1893

EXCERPT FROM "THE SIGNIFICANCE OF THE FRONTIER IN AMERICAN HISTORY"

Frederick Jackson Turner

In a recent bulletin of the Superintendent of the Census for 1890 appear these significant words: "Up to and including 1880 the country had a frontier of settlement, but at present the unsettled area has been so broken into by isolated bodies of settlement that there can hardly be said to be a frontier line. In the discussion of its extent, its westward movement, etc., it can not, therefore, any longer have a place in the census reports." This brief official statement marks the closing of a great historic movement. Up to our own day American history has been in a large degree the history of the colonization of the Great West. The existence of an area of free land, its continuous recession, and the advance of American settlement westward, explain American development. . . .

[This] development has exhibited not merely advance along a single line, but a return to primitive conditions on a continually advancing frontier line, and a new development for that area. American social development has been continually beginning over again on the frontier. This perennial rebirth, this fluidity of American life, this expansion westward with its new opportunities, its continuous touch with the simplicity of primitive society, furnish the forces dominating American character. . . .

The frontier is the line of most rapid and effective Americanization. The wilderness masters the colonist. It finds him a European in dress, industries, tools, modes of travel, and thought. It takes him from the railroad car and puts him in a birch canoe. It strips off the garments of civilization and arrays him in the hunting shirt and the moccasin. It puts him in the log cabin of the Cherokee and Iroquois and runs an Indian palisade around him. Before long he has gone to planting Indian corn and plowing with a sharp stick; he shouts the war cry and takes the scalp in orthodox Indian fashion. In short, at the frontier the environment is at first too strong for the man. He must accept the conditions which it furnishes, or perish. . . . Little by little he transforms the wilderness, but the outcome is not the old Europe, not simply the development of Germanic germs. . . . The fact is, that here is a new product that is American. . . .

The Atlantic frontier was compounded of fisherman, fur-trader, miner, cattle-raiser, and farmer. Excepting the fisherman, each type of industry was on the march toward the West, impelled by an irresistible attraction. Each passed in successive waves across the continent. Stand at the Cumberland Gap and watch the procession of civilization, marching single file—the buffalo following the trail to the salt springs, the Indian, the fur-trader and hunter, the cattle-raiser, the pioneer farmer—and the frontier has passed by. Stand at South Pass in the Rockies a century later and see the same procession with wider intervals between. . . .

The most important effect of the frontier has been in the promotion of democracy here and in Europe. . . . The frontier is productive of individualism. Complex society is precipitated by the wilderness into a kind of primitive organization based on the family. The tendency is anti-social. It produces antipathy to control, and particularly to any direct control. The tax-gatherer is viewed as a representative of oppression. . . . To the frontier the American intellect owes its striking characteristics. That coarseness and strength combined with acuteness and inquisitiveness; that practical, inventive turn of mind, quick to find expedients; that masterful grasp of material things, lacking in the artistic but powerful to effect great ends; that restless, nervous energy; that dominant individualism, working for good and for evil, and withal that buoyancy and exuberance which comes with freedom—these are traits of the frontier, or traits called out elsewhere because of the existence of the frontier. Since the days when the fleet of Columbus sailed into the waters of the New World, America has been another name for opportunity. . . . What the Mediterranean Sea was to the Greeks, breaking the bond of custom, offering new experiences, calling out new institutions and activities, that, and more, the ever retreating frontier has been to the United States directly, and to the nations of Europe more remotely. And now, four centuries from the discovery of America, at the end of a hundred years of life under the Constitution, the frontier has gone, and with its going has closed the first period of American history.

parents from upper New York state, he was reared in a land fringed by the interminable forest and still stamped with the mark of youth. There he mingled with pioneers who had trapped beaver or hunted Indians or cleared the virgin wilderness; from them he learned something of the free and easy democratic values prevailing among those who judged men by their own accomplishments rather than those of their ancestors. At the University of Wisconsin Turner's faith in cultural democracy was deepened, while his intellectual vistas were widened through contact with teachers who led him into that wonderland of adventure where scientific techniques were being applied to social problems, where Darwin's evolutionary hypothesis was awakening scholars to the continuity of progress, and where searchers after truth were beginning to realize the multiplicity of forces responsible for human behavior. The young student showed how well he had learned these lessons in his master's essay on "The Character and Influence of the Fur Trade in Wisconsin"; he emphasized the evolution of institutions from simple to complex forms.

From Wisconsin Turner journeyed to Johns Hopkins University, as did many eager young scholars of that day, only to meet stubborn opposition for the historical theories already taking shape in his mind. His principal professor, Herbert Baxter Adams, viewed mankind's development in evolutionary terms, but held that environment had no place in the equation; American institutions could be understood only as outgrowths of European "germs" that had originated among Teutonic tribes in the forests of medieval Germany. To Turner this explanation was unsatisfactory. The "germ theory" explained the similarities between Europe and America, but what of the many differences? This problem was still much in his mind when he returned to the University of Wisconsin as an instructor in 1889. In two remarkable papers prepared during the next few years he set forth his answer. The first, "The Significance of History," reiterated his belief in what historians call "multiple causation"; to understand man's complex nature, he insisted, one needed not only a knowledge of past politics, but a familiarity with social, economic, and cultural forces as well. The second, "Problems in American History," attempted to isolate those forces most influential in explaining the unique features of American development. Among these Turner believed that the most important was the need for institutions to "adapt themselves to the changes of a remarkably developing, expanding people."

This was the theory that was expanded into a full-blown historical hypothesis in the famous essay on "The Significance of the Frontier in American History," read at a conference of historians held in connection with the World Fair in Chicago in 1893. The differences between European and American civilization, Turner stated in that monumental work, were in part the product of the distinctive environment of the New World. The most unusual features of that environment were "the existence of an area of free land, its continuous recession, and the advance of American settlement westward." This free land served as a magnet to draw men westward, attracted by the hope of economic gain or adventure. They came as Europeans or easterners, but they soon realized that the wilderness environment was ill-adapted to the habits, institutions, and cultural baggage of the stratified societies they had left behind. Complex political institutions were unnecessary in a tiny frontier outpost; traditional economic practices were useless in an isolated community geared to an economy of self-sufficiency; rigid social customs were outmoded in a land where prestige depended on skill with the axe or rifle rather than on hereditary glories; cultural pursuits were unessential in a land where so many material tasks awaited doing. Hence in each pioneer settlement there occurred a rapid reversion to the primitive. What little government was necessary was provided by simple associations of settlers; each man looked after his family without reliance on his fellows; social hierarchies disintegrated, and cultural progress came to a halt. As the newcomers moved backward along the scale of civilization, the habits and customs of their traditional cultures were forgotten.

Gradually, however, newcomers drifted in, and as the man-land ratio increased, the community began a slow climb back toward civilization. Governmental controls were tightened and extended, economic specialization began, social stratification set in, and cultural activities quickened. But the new society that eventually emerged differed from the old from which it had sprung. The abandonment of cultural baggage during the migrations, the borrowings from the many cultures represented in each pioneer settlement, the deviations natural in separate evolutions, and the impact of the environment all played their parts in creating a unique social organism similar to but differing from those in the East. An "Americanization" of men and their institutions had taken place.

Turner believed that many of the characteristics associated with the American people were traceable to their experience, during the three centuries required to settle the continent, of constantly "beginning over again." Their mobility, their optimism, their inventiveness and willingness to accept innovation, their materialism, their exploitive wastefulness—these were frontier traits; for the pioneer, accustomed to repeated moves as he drifted westward, viewed the world through rose-colored glasses as he dreamed of a better future, experimented constantly as he adapted artifacts and customs to his peculiar environment, scorned culture as a deterrent to the practical tasks that bulked so large in his life, and squandered seemingly inexhaustible natural resources with abandon. Turner also ascribed America's distinctive brand of individualism, with its dislike of governmental interference in economic functions, to the experience of pioneers who wanted no hindrance from society as they exploited nature's riches. Similarly, he traced the exaggerated nationalism of the United States to its roots among frontiersmen who looked to the national government for land, transportation outlets, and protection against the Indians. And he believed that America's faith in democracy had stemmed from a pioneering experience in which the leveling influence of poverty and the uniqueness of local problems encouraged majority self-rule. He pointed out that these characteristics, prominent among frontiersmen, had persisted long after the frontier itself was no more.

This was Turner's famous "frontier hypothesis." For a generation after its enunciation its persuasive logic won uncritical acceptance among historians, but beginning in the late 1920's, and increasingly after Turner's death in 1932, an avalanche of criticism steadily mounted. His theories, critics said, were contradictory, his generalizations unsupported, his assumptions inadequately based; what empirical proof could he advance, they asked, to prove that the frontier experience was responsible for American individualism, mobility, or wastefulness? He was damned as a romanticist for his claim that democracy sprang from the forest environment of the United States and as an isolationist for failing to recognize the continuing impact of Europe on America. As the "bait-Turner" vogue gained popularity among younger scholars of the 1930's with their international, semi-Marxian views of history, the criticisms of the frontier theory

became as irrational as the earlier support rendered it by overenthusiastic advocates.

During the past decade, however, a healthy reaction has slowly and unspectacularly gained momentum. Today's scholars, gradually realizing that Turner was advancing a hypothesis rather than proving a theory, have shown a healthy tendency to abandon fruitless haggling over the meaning of his phrases and to concentrate instead on testing his assumptions. They have directed their efforts primarily toward re-examining his hypothesis in the light of criticisms directed against it and applying it to frontier areas beyond the borders of the United States. Their findings have modified

These two photographs of the same pioneer couple, the Ephraim Swain Finches, show how rapidly change came to the frontier. Above, the Finches stand before

many of the views expressed by Turner but have gone far toward proving that the frontier hypothesis remains one essential tool—albeit not the only one—for interpreting American history.

That Turner was guilty of oversimplifying both the nature and the causes of the migration process was certainly true. He pictured settlers as moving westward in an orderly procession—fur trappers, cattlemen, miners, pioneer farmers, and equipped farmers—with each group playing its part in the transmutation of a wilderness into a civilization. Free land was the magnet that lured them onward, he believed, and this operated most effectively in periods of depression, when the displaced workers of the East sought a refuge from economic storms amidst nature's abundance in the West. "The wilderness ever opened the gate of escape to the poor, the discontented and oppressed," Turner wrote at one time. "If social conditions tended to crystallize in the east, beyond the Alleghenies there was freedom."

No one of these assumptions can be substantiated in the simplified form in which Turner stated it. His vision of an "orderly procession of civilization, marching single file westward" failed to account for deviations that were almost as important as the norm; as essential to the conquest of the forest as trappers or farmers were soldiers, mill-operators, distillers, artisans, storekeepers, merchants, lawyers, editors, specu-

the mayor reduced to a mere figurehead.

The pioneers who marched westward in this disorganized procession were not attracted by the magnet of "free land," for Turner's assumption that before 1862 the public domain was open to all who could pay $1.25 an acre, or that acreage was free after the Homestead Act was passed in that year, has been completely disproved. Turner failed to recognize the presence in the procession to the frontier of that omnipresent profit-seeker, the speculator. Jobbers were always ahead of farmers in the advance westward, buying up likely town sites or appropriating the best farm lands, where the soil was good and transportation outlets available. When the settler arrived his choice was between paying the speculator's price or accepting an inferior site. Even the Homestead Act failed to lessen speculative activity. Capitalizing on generous government grants to railroads and state educational institutions (which did not want to be bothered with sales to individuals), or buying bonus script from soldiers, or securing Indian lands as the reservations were contracted, or seizing on faulty features of congressional acts for the disposal of swampland and timberland, jobbers managed to engross most of the Far West's arable acreage. As a result, for every newcomer who obtained a homestead from the government, six or seven purchased farms from speculators.

their log-and-mud hut in Nebraska in the 1880's; twenty years later, prospering, they built a sturdy frame house, complete with scroll-saw decorations.

lators, and town dwellers. All played their role, and all contributed to a complex frontier social order that bore little resemblance to the primitive societies Turner pictured. This was especially the case with the early town builders. The hamlets that sprang up adjacent to each pioneer settlement were products of the environment as truly as were the cattlemen or Indian fighters; each evolved economic functions geared to the needs of the primitive area surrounding it, and, in the tight public controls maintained over such essential functions as grist-milling or retail selling, each mirrored the frontiersmen's community-oriented views. In these villages, too, the equalitarian influence of the West was reflected in thoroughly democratic governments, with popularly elected councils supreme and

Those who made these purchases were not, as Turner believed, displaced eastern workers fleeing periodic industrial depressions. Few city-dwelling artisans had the skills or inclination, and almost none the capital, to escape to the frontier. Land prices of $1.25 an acre may seem low today, but they were prohibitive for laborers earning only a dollar a day. Moreover, needed farm machinery, animals, and housing added about $1,000 to the cost of starting a farm in the 1850's, while the cheapest travel rate from New York to St. Louis was about $13 a person. Because these sums were always beyond the reach of factory workers (in bad times they deterred migration even from the rural East), the

CONTINUED ON PAGE 86

The CANNY CAYUSE

The white man made certain his

imported thoroughbred could outrun

the red man's pony, but the Indian chief

was wise in the gambler's ways

Among the Indians of the Plains and the Rocky Mountains the sport of horse racing was a product of necessity and passion—the necessity of mastering the breeding of the horse, on which their very lives depended, and a passion, seemingly inborn, for gambling. Wherever they came together—with other Indians or with friendly white men of sporting blood—horse racing became the principal social event.

The Umatilla and Cayuse tribes had since 1853 lived on the same reservation in northeastern Oregon. When they crossbred the horses they had acquired from other tribes with animals obtained from white men who came through their country, the result was a pony that was small, tough, and fast.

In 1875, A. B. Meacham, just finishing a six-year term as superintendent of Indian Affairs in Oregon, published a now-forgotten book called Wigwam and War Path. *In it I found the following account of a horse race in which white men tried to cheat their Cayuse adversaries—with results that were wholly unforeseen.* —John Clark Hunt

How-lish-wam-po, chief of the Cayuse, is the owner of several thousand horses. He is a stout-built man, has a dark complexion, wears his hair just clear of his shoulders, and is now past middle age. He is a natural horseman and a match for any man of any race in matters pertaining to horses. He is really king of the turf in the Umatilla country.

The racing habits of these people are well known, and many a white man has found them more than his match. A white man named Joe Crabb once imported a horse for the express purpose of taking everything the Indians had. He made known his desire to race, and he soon found opportunity for an investment. The preliminaries were arranged: the race was to be run over the Indian racecourse, which was located on the bottom lands of the Umatilla river. The turf was smooth and level, and the track was over two miles and a half in length.

At one end of this course a post was planted, round which the racers were to turn and come back to the starting point, making a distance of a little over five miles and a quarter.

Joe Crabb had been present at a race months before, when, unbeknown to Crabb, How-lish-wam-po had *permitted* his horse to be beaten; and as Crabb had measured the distance, recorded the winner's time, and subsequently tested the speed of his own horse against it, he felt he had a sure thing.

The white men came with groom and riders, making a camp near the Indians and standing guard over their own horse, to prevent accident. The Indians were not so careful of their horse (at least Joe Crabb thought they were not), and, since everything is fair in gambling as in war, he decided to *know* for himself how the speed of these two horses would compare. He thought, as thousands of other white men have, that it was no harm to cheat an Injun, no matter by what means.

There is a general belief that Indians sleep when their eyes are shut, and especially just before daylight. Sending a careful, trusty man to get the Indian horse (leaving another in its place), Crabb led the two horses out on the prairie and made a few trials of speed between them. The result was satisfactory. He found that his horse was able to outdistance the other.

Now How-lish-wam-po owned two horses which looked very nearly alike, one the racer, the other half-brother to him, but not so fleet. They were pintos—spotted horses—so the deception was complete.

The Indian horses are never stabled, groomed, shod, or grain-fed. Their system of training differs very much from that the white man uses. After a race is agreed upon, the animal is tied up to a stake or tree.

This painting by George Catlin shows the first stage in Indian horse-training—catching and taming the wild pony. These Indians are Comanches of the southern plains, whose horses, Catlin said, were small and powerful, "with an exceedingly prominent eye, sharp nose, high nostril, small foot and delicate leg." Their unkempt appearance belied their great speed.

If he is fat, they starve him down, giving him only water. If, however, he is in good condition, they lead him out to grass an hour or so each day, and at nightfall they run him over the course.

In this instance the half-brother was tied up and left unguarded, with the hope that Crabb would steal him out and try his speed. Sure enough, he fell into the trap that How-lish-wam-po set for him. The real race horse was miles away, under proper training. The fame of this wonderful winner had spread far and wide, as did the news of the approaching contest.

When the morning of the race arrived, the roads leading to the valley of the Umatilla gave full proof of the interest the people of the surrounding country had in this important affair.

They came from places several hundred miles distant and from the settlements surrounding the Reservation. The little towns furnished their quota, and the farmers excused themselves for going, hoping, as they told their wives at home, that they should meet with someone with whom they had business. Through various devices nearly every man, and a part of the women also, found excuse to be there. People who never gambled with dollars, and would blush to own they were fast people, found their way to the Umatilla.

The racecourse, which I have described, was parallel with a low range of grassy hills that rose by gentle slopes from the valley to an altitude of fifty to one hundred feet. Long before the time for the race, carriages, buggies, wagons, and horses might be seen standing on the hills or driving over the greensward, while at the standing point was assembled a great motley crowd, on foot and on horseback. The Indians were in their gala-day dress—paints, feathers, long hair, red blankets; in fact, it was a dress parade for white and red men alike.

The manner of betting at an Indian horse race differs somewhat from affairs of the kind among white men. One man is selected as a stakeholder for all the money bets. Horses that are wagered are tied together and put in the care of Indian boys. Other stakes—coats, blankets, saddles, pistols, knives, and all kinds of personal effects—are thrown into a common heap and tied together.

As the starting hour approaches, two judges are elected—one white man and one Indian. (Two are re-

CONTINUED ON PAGE 92

11

WHEN PERRY UNLOCKED

Throughout the mid-1830's there raged in American naval circles, as well as in Congress when defense appropriations came up, a debate on the wisdom of introducing into our sail-driven frigate fleet a revolutionary new method of propulsion—steam. Most captains as well as congressmen were opposed to the innovation. It was costly. It was uncertain. Sailors knew nothing about machinery and did not want to learn. There had even been a near-mutiny when a Navy crew refused to hoist out firebox clinkers from an experimental floating battery designed by Fulton.

Finally an aggressive four-striper, respected as the younger brother of Commodore Oliver Hazard Perry of 1812 fame and as a tough quarter-deck sundowner and innovator in his own right, used the influence of his name and family to help

THE "GATE OF THE SUN"

Japan's feudal, shut-in history

suddenly came to an end

when the bluff American commodore

dropped anchor in Tokyo Bay

By WILLIAM HARLAN HALE

Perry first landed in Japan (left) at Kurihama, a tiny village at the entrance to Tokyo Bay, on July 14, 1853. The event was recorded by his official artist, Wilhelm Heine. Evidently the Japanese who carved the statuette of the Commodore at right had never seen a Western-style chair: Perry's legs are this one's only support in the front.

persuade Congress to authorize two experimental vessels. One of these was launched as U.S.S. *Mississippi,* a hybrid sail-and-steam frigate one-third larger than the hallowed *Constitution* and mounting, under her canvas and above her thrashing paddle wheels, ten huge pivot guns. The ship and her promoter and first commander, Matthew Calbraith Perry, were destined together for a unique place in world history.

Broad-beamed, she was fast and steady in all weathers—a deep-sea cruiser of a range and power phenomenal in those days. At Vera Cruz in the Mexican War her guns, firing new-style explosive shells rather than conventional ball, silenced the harbor forts in short order when Perry took her in close. She became the showpiece of the United States Navy, presenting her black topsides at ports around the world in over a quarter-million miles of cruising. For his part the formidable Perry—now a commodore as his brother had been—became the Navy's reigning hero. So it was fitting that just this ship and just this commander should set out together on still another mission, for which this time there was no precedent—the effort of the U.S. government in 1853 to open by massive persuasion the gates of Japan, hitherto hermetically sealed. Who could tell: the *Mississippi*'s big guns might again come in handy.

In the first days of that July, Nipponese fishermen working the midsummer waters off Honshu in their bobbing junks met a startling sight. Four American men-of-war, two bearing sail and two making thick, ominous smoke, came plowing toward the forbidden coast at Cape Sagami, within sight of the mists that veiled sacred Mount Fuji. In the van, big wheels churning and guns run out, steered the *Mississippi* and the *Susquehanna*, the latter flying the Commodore's broad pennant. The squadron was heavily freighted with two years' provisions, a cargo of gifts (including even a miniature railway), interpreters, wines, liquors, ammunition, small arms, cutlasses, and an embossed letter of friendship from President Millard Fillmore to the Emperor of Japan.

Aboard the squadron, as it approached the gnarled shores where such things as buoys, lights, beacons, pilots, or reliable charts were unknown, everything was taut and ship-shape. This was to be expected under Old Matt Perry, for he was famed as the Navy's leading disciplinarian. Bayard Taylor, a handsome young world traveler and roving reporter of Horace Greeley's New York *Tribune*, who had been taken aboard at Hong Kong and given the temporary rank of master's mate in order to help write up the expedition's story, told of the stiff drill required of the crews by their gravel-voiced commodore: the daily calls to general quarters amid empty seas; the drum rolls and fife calls summoning all hands to run out guns, repel imaginary boarders, and rig pumps to douse hypothetical fires; the roar of topside commands over nonexistent battle smoke; and the bands ordered to play "Yankee Doodle" after simulated victories over Oriental attackers who had not materialized.

All that actually met the mighty expedition were those few frightened fishermen. "As the squadron sailed up the coast," the official narrative has it, "eight or ten junks hove into sight, and two or three of them were observed soon to change their course and to turn back toward the shore, as if to announce the arrival of strangers. . . . The *Mississippi*, in spite of a wind, moved on with all sails furled at the rate of eight or nine knots, much to the astonishment of the crews of Japanese fishing junks . . . who stood up in their boats and were evidently expressing the liveliest surprise at the sight of the first steamer ever beheld in Japanese waters."

Then the black-hulled squadron, with leadsmen in the chains, moved slowly into the strait that leads into Yedo Bay [now Tokyo Bay], while mists lifted from the rice paddies, villages, and ridges on either side. Angry guard boats ornamented with black tassels swarmed about. The flagship made a signal: "Have no communication with shore: allow none from shore." Anchors rattled out as the ships came in line abreast of the narrows. In the moment when the echoes died away, all Japan's age-old, shut-in history suddenly ended, to be followed by another chapter—one that in turn was to close just 92 years later when another American warship, over twenty times the bulk of Perry's side-

TEXT CONTINUED ON PAGE 94

14

JAPAN'S FIRST LONG LOOK AT THE WEST: A PORTFOLIO

Wherever they went in Japan, Perry and his men were surrounded by little knots of Japanese so curious that, not content with merely looking, they repeatedly pulled out their mulberry-bark paper, India ink, and hair pencils to make notes and sketches. "Every man," said Perry's official narrative, "seemed anxious to try his skill at drawing." On the next nine pages is a portfolio of the results. It constitutes a charming Oriental view, sophisticated yet full of wonder, of a civilization completely unknown to the artists. Some of these paintings were presented to Bishop James DeWolf Perry, the Commodore's great-grandnephew, when he made a missionary tour of Japan in 1933, and are in the collection of the Bishop's son, the Reverend DeWolf Perry of Charleston, S.C. To him, to the Norfolk (Virginia) Museum, and to the Library of Congress we express our appreciation for help in assembling the portfolio. It begins (at right) with a wood-block drawing by the famous artist Hiroshige of one of Perry's "black ships," probably done in March of 1854, when the Commodore, his squadron greatly augmented since its first landing the previous summer, dropped anchor off Yokohama to negotiate a Japanese-American treaty of friendship and trade.

TENSIONS EASE BETWEEN SHIP AND SHORE, AND PERRY

When Perry first went ashore at Yokohama on March 8, mutual Japanese-American suspicions were still strong. The Commodore armed even his accompanying bandsmen with pistols and cutlasses, and his hosts had all U.S. shore parties closely watched. As negotiations progressed, however, the tension abated, and American officers began to go on sight-seeing excursions (above). In the towns, to Perry's annoyance, a Japanese attendant would scurry ahead to "order the women and the rabble to keep out of the way." Protesting, Perry was told that Japanese women were too modest to look upon a stranger, but he was not so gullible as to believe this: the members of one of his coast-surveying parties had already received some obvious solicitations. Perry found the citizens of Yokohama "thriving and contented," the girls "well formed and pretty," and social life just as brisk as in America. On their part, the Japanese were intensely curious about the foreigners. They examined the sailors' uniforms closely and even begged for the shiny gold buttons on the officers' tunics. This minute observation is evident in their detailed sketches (right) of Commodore Perry and several of his chief officers.

Interpreter S. W. Williams

横濱外國人行列之圖

一川芳員画

GOES SIGHT-SEEING

ommander Henry Adams   Commodore Perry   Interpreter H. Portman   Lt. Oliver Hazard Perry   Captain Joel Abbott

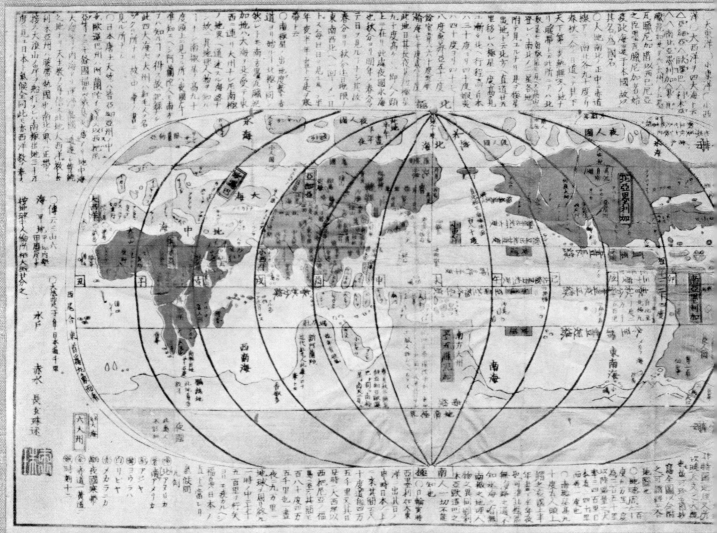

This map of the world, drawn late in the eighteenth century by the famous cartographer Nagakubo Sekisui of Mito, was still in circulation in Japan when Perry arrived. It is comparatively accurate as to the relative size and location of Japan and the United States, but the continental contours are greatly distorted and Sekisui was vague about the polar regions. The north he calls "country of the night people"; of the south he says, "It is impossible to know about this place."

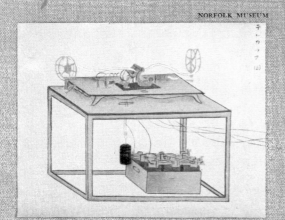

A Japanese sketch of the telegraph transmitter.

A U.S. officer, reportedly Major Gillen, drills a detachment of marines.

AMERICAN

TECHNOLOGY

AND

MILITARY

METHODS

AMAZE

THE

JAPANESE

If the Japanese were curious about American dress and manners, they were astonished at some of their visitors' mechanical devices. These, because Japan had been so long cut off from the world, were virtually unknown to them. Of paramount interest were the steam frigates of Perry's squadron. Of one of them, probably the Mississippi (below), the artist wrote (as translated by a Japanese): "The name of boat is steam ship or fire wheel ship. . . . She don't care a tempest, heavy rain nor violent waves, she runs as quick as a dragon in swimming." A telegraph transmitter (lower left, opposite page) which was among Perry's gifts fascinated the Japanese. In his Black Ships Off Japan Arthur Walworth describes how they helped the Americans string a wire between two buildings and were surprised that, no matter how fast they ran the half-mile interval, the message always got there first. The commissioners also showed enthusiasm for the drill of Perry's marines, who "marched and countermarched over the rough stones," wrote a U.S. officer, "until I thought that Prince Hayashi would have the ague whenever he should hereafter meet a marine, and finally ended their evolutions by coming within fifteen paces of the crowd, and snapping their muskets in a volley direct at their noble highnesses' dough bags."

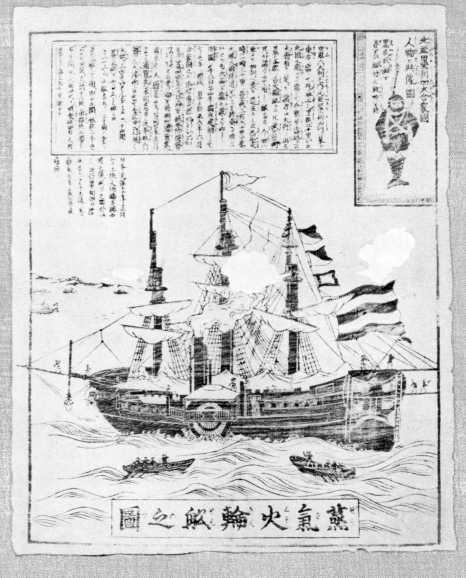

Perry and his standard-bearer come ashore.

JAPANESE WRESTLERS, AMERICAN MINSTRELS ENLIVEN

テレガラフ園

全軆舞園

THE TREATY-MAKING

After the manner of treaty-makers and plenipotentiaries throughout history, Commodore Perry and his Japanese hosts entertained one another lavishly. The Japanese staged the first social event, in response to the presentation of American gifts. Twenty-five monstrous wrestlers were paraded outside the treaty house, and nothing would do but that the Commodore should feel the muscles and punch the paunch of the mightiest of them (opposite page, bottom), Koyanagi, "the reputed bully of the capital." Next the wrestlers engaged in a test of strength: with ease they hoisted the 125-pound sacks of rice on their backs; efforts to duplicate the feat left the Americans with their tongues hanging out. A few days later, as the negotiations neared their end, Perry reciprocated by inviting the Japanese delegates to a convivial feast aboard his flagship, following it with a minstrel show (above and below) staged by American sailors. It completely captivated the Japanese audience. "When the sable gentlemen made their appearance," a midshipman later wrote, "a murmur of astonishment arose among our simple guests. . . . I thought the commissioners would have died with their suppressed laughter (for they never laughed out as we do)." Afterward, having partaken liberally of Perry's foods, wines, and whiskies, the guests departed, one of them clasping Perry in a boozy embrace (crushing the Commodore's new epaulets) and saying, "Japan and America, all the same heart." As Perry's interpreter, S. Wells Williams, noted in his diary: "It is not for want of cumshaws to the Japanese that we shall fail of making a treaty, especially drinkables of all sorts."

A LILLIPUTIAN LOCOMOTIVE DELIGHTS PERRY'S HOSTS

横濱海岸鉄道蒸氣車圖

Of all the American gifts none made a greater hit with the Japanese than a quarter-scale steam railroad, complete with engine, tender, passenger car, and 370 feet of track. Here it is seen against a backdrop of Yokohama Harbor filled with Perry's ships. This picture, like the first in this portfolio, was drawn on wood blocks by Hiroshige; reproductions of it were sold to Japanese tourists as souvenirs of Yokohama. The artist, who has labeled the passenger car with the Japanese characters for "middle class," has exaggerated the size of the train. Actually, it was so small that not even the diminutive Japanese could squeeze inside. Not to be cheated of a ride, they perched on the roof; according to Perry's official narrative, "It was a spectacle not a little ludicrous to behold a dignified mandarin whirling around the circular road at the rate of twenty miles an hour, with his loose robes flying in the wind." The spectacle was repeated in other Japanese ports which Perry visited. Then, having accomplished his mission, he sailed triumphantly for home.

Did the President, as he claimed, lose a battle but win a war in his attempt to pack the Supreme Court? Historical perspective suggests another answer

F.D.R. vs. the Supreme Court

Roosevelt confers with Senator Robinson, his lieutenant in the fight. "This bill's raising hell in the Senate," Robinson reported.

By MERLO J. PUSEY

The great struggle between the President and the Supreme Court in 1937 stirred the national emotions to unusual depths because it brought Franklin D. Roosevelt's crusade against depression into collision with one of our most hallowed traditions. And after a lapse of twenty years it remains high on the list of the most dramatic contests in our constitutional history.

In the first phase of the struggle, beginning in 1935, the court invalidated a large part of the New Deal. The effect was to bring down upon its head the wrath of the country as well as that of the White House. In the second phase, two years later, Roosevelt moved against the court more boldly and directly than any other President had ever done. Public opinion then swung to the defense of the court, and F. D. R. suffered the most humiliating defeat of his career. Yet the final outcome was a victory for liberal interpretation of the Constitution as well as for independence of the judiciary. The crash assault failed, and moderation won.

To understand the intensity of the struggle, it must be remembered that in the middle thirties the country was still trying to climb out of its depression storm cellar. In 1933 Roosevelt had come to power with the banks closed and the economy thoroughly demoralized. He had ushered in an almost revolutionary concept of government stewardship over the national economy. With the co-operation of a frightened Congress, he had devalued the dollar and placed industry under a system of codes and agriculture under production quotas. He had created various other "new instruments of power," initiated sweeping social reforms, and given organized labor the greatest impetus it had ever experienced.

The President's courage and industry were contagious. While the people applauded, Congress worked with feverish haste to enact almost every bill that the White House "brain trust" produced. Some of this outpouring of reform and recovery legislation has survived and become a distinctive part of our national heritage. But many of the early emergency bills, in addition to being highly experimental in nature, were poorly drafted. The men around the President realized that some of their ventures could scarcely be reconciled with the Constitution as it was then interpreted by the Supreme Court. But in their haste they passed lightly over this aspect of their problem. A new era was dawning. Its methods and objectives could not be judged by the outmoded criteria of the past. Many of the New Dealers concluded that, in any event, the Supreme Court would not dare to upset statutes on which the nation's recovery from its worst depression seemed to depend.

The rude awakening from this illusion came early in 1935, when the Supreme Court invalidated the National Recovery Administration's petroleum code as an unconstitutional venture into executive law-making. Soon there followed Chief Justice Charles Evans Hughes's opinion, written on behalf of a unanimous court, which wiped out the whole NRA and its progeny of Blue Eagles. [In the case before the court (commonly called the "sick chicken" case), four brothers named Schechter had been found guilty of marketing diseased fowl in violation of the NRA's poultry code. Their lawyers contended only that Congress had no power to regulate local—as distinguished from interstate—business, but the court went beyond this and invalidated the whole industrial recovery act. As Fred Rodell wrote in *Nine Men:* "A few sick chickens had murdered the mighty Blue Eagle."] The court found the NRA wanting on two counts: first, Congress had delegated extensive law-making powers to trade organizations acting with the approval of the President; second, it had swept under federal control wholly local activities—in this instance the marketing of poultry—

only remotely related to the interstate commerce which Congress is authorized to regulate.

On the same "Black Monday" the court unanimously struck down the Frazier-Lemke Act for relief of farm debtors, with Justice Louis D. Brandeis writing the opinion, and reversed the President's dismissal of William E. Humphrey from the quasi-judicial Federal Trade Commission. The Humphrey decision is said to have nettled the President more than any other, but when he held a lengthy press conference and denounced the Supreme Court for taking the country back to a "horse-and-buggy" concept of interstate commerce it was the NRA decision that he had in mind.

Actually the court's *coup de grâce* to the NRA was a blessing in disguise to the Roosevelt administration, for its unwieldy codes were already cracking up. The court saved the President from what would have been an embarrassing retreat. But F. D. R. saw in the sweeping nature of the "sick chicken" decision a threat to other parts of his program, and in this he was right.

In most of the early New Deal cases the court had been unanimous, but as it moved on to more controversial issues its long-standing internal schism was much in evidence. On the conservative side, Justices Willis Van Devanter, Pierce Butler, George Sutherland, and James C. McReynolds nearly always stood together. To them any innovation was likely to appear as an unconstitutional seizure of power. The liberal wing, consisting of Justices Brandeis, Harlan F. Stone,

The Court, 1937

Owen J. Roberts   Pierce Butler   Harlan Fiske Stone   Benjamin N. Cardozo

Louis D. Brandeis   Willis Van Devanter   Charles Evans Hughes   James C. McReynolds   George Sutherland

and Benjamin N. Cardozo, was more inclined to give Congress a free rein unless it had flagrantly overreached the limits of its power. Chief Justice Hughes occupied a middle ground, and Justice Owen J. Roberts often stood with him. For the New Deal, the result was fluctuation between reverses and narrow victories.

The court's action in the "gold clause" case in the spring of 1935 both relieved and angered the President. In this decision, four associate justices stood with Hughes in condemning Congress' repudiation of the government's promise to redeem its bonds and currency in gold. But, having thus bowed to principle, the court saved the economy from catastrophe by ruling that bondholders, who had suffered no loss of purchasing power when Congress increased the value of gold in terms of paper dollars, could not hold the government to its promise to pay in gold or its equivalent. From this latter part of the decision the four conservatives dissented. For the moment, the ingenious solution Hughes had invented to save the government from a crushing addition to its debt averted an open clash between the President and the court, for F. D. R. had prepared a radio address announcing his refusal to enforce the decision—an address to be delivered if the court should allow the bondholders to take their pound of flesh.

Another New Deal innovation, the Agricultural Adjustment Administration, might have been saved had Congress, in building the AAA, used its power to regulate interstate commerce. Instead, it had used its taxing power. Hughes, Roberts, and the four conservatives concluded that the benefit payments to farmers, financed by a processing tax, had the effect of coercing them into compliance with a regulatory scheme that had no relation to interstate commerce. Stone and his liberal brethren dissented with unusual vehemence, and subsequent judicial thinking tends to support their conclusions if not the bite in Stone's words.

Both court factions broke away from Hughes's middle ground in the case involving the Guffey Act, designed to rescue the ailing coal industry. Hughes thought the price-fixing section of this statute was valid and that only its labor provisions were constitutionally defective. But a majority of five swept the whole act into the discard, with Brandeis, Stone, and Cardozo dissenting. The Municipal Bankruptcy Act met a similar fate.

Finally, the same majority of five released a legal block-buster by striking down New York State's minimum wage law for women. Coming on the heels of many decisions rejecting the extension of federal power over the economy, this restriction of state power seemed to indicate that *no* government could legally cope with the grave problems of the depression. The court's extreme stand-pattism raised an outcry throughout the land. Dissenting opinions by Hughes and Stone, in which Brandeis and Cardozo joined, pointedly disclosed the alarm felt within the court itself over this reactionary trend.

The white-bearded Chief Justice, whose liberal instincts were neatly blended with a high regard for traditional constitutionalism, was almost as much concerned over this turn of events as was the President. Both brooded on how to save the country from the consequences of static legalism. But, while Hughes thought in terms of correcting loosely drawn legislation and interpreting the basic law more liberally, Roosevelt turned toward more drastic measures.

Soon after the NRA decisions in 1935, F. D. R. had put his attorney general, Homer Cummings, to work on "the court problem." In the following months the Department of Justice and the President quietly studied the respective merits of a constitutional amendment broadening federal powers, a statute limiting the court's jurisdiction, a provision requiring a two-thirds vote in the court to nullify an act of Congress, and an enlargement of the court's membership. No conclusions were drawn, however, and the issue was astutely avoided in the 1936 presidential campaign, except for a pledge in the Democratic platform that the economic and social problems of the day would be met in a constitutional manner. Republican charges that the President, if re-elected, would resort to the "tyranny" of court-packing met with impassioned Democratic denials.

Once Roosevelt's towering victory over Governor Alfred M. Landon was achieved, however, he moved against the court with supreme confidence. Did he not have a new mandate from the people to carry out his New Deal? Was not the court standing in his way? To Roosevelt's way of thinking, his chief problem was to find the most effective way of clearing this obstruction from his path.

It was Cummings who finally came up with the idea of naming new judges to replace the aged men on the bench. The fact that Justice McReynolds, when he had been attorney general in 1913, had advanced such a plan for driving overage judges of the lower courts into retirement made this approach irresistible. To the President's delight, Cummings shrewdly camouflaged the scheme in the trimmings of judicial reform. With the aid of a few trusted lieutenants, he drafted and redrafted a bill and a presidential message to Congress.

There was no discussion of the bill with the Cabinet, congressional leaders, or members of the court. F. D. R. gave his annual dinner for the judiciary on the evening of February 3, 1937, without breathing a

Chief Justice Hughes was a most formidable opponent. His very appearance—dignified, even Olympian—helped rally public confidence in the court and defeat the President.

word of his secret to the judges. On the morning of February 5 he disclosed the contents of his message to an incredulous group of Cabinet and congressional leaders a few minutes before he jubilantly explained it to the press. Both his aloofness in working out the plan and his manner of presenting it suggested that he regarded it as almost a *fait accompli*.

The President represented his bill as a reform aimed at correcting injustice and relieving the court of congestion. His inference was that aged justices on the Supreme Court bench were keeping their calendar clear by rejecting an excessive number of petitions for review—a charge that almost every lawyer knew to be false. Though he called for a "persistent infusion of new blood" into the judiciary, there was only a vague hint of the bill's real purpose in his suggestion that it would obviate the need for more fundamental changes in the powers of the courts or in the Constitution.

The heart of the bill was the provision giving the President authority to name an additional federal judge for every incumbent who had been on the bench ten years and had not resigned within six months after reaching the age of seventy. As six members of the Supreme Court had passed that age limit, F. D. R. could immediately have appointed six new justices. If Chief Justice Hughes and his five aged associates had chosen to remain, the membership of the court would have been enlarged from nine to fifteen.

Legislators gasped over the boldness of the plan, yet many of them gave it immediate support. Others who dared to speak out against it assumed their opposition would be futile; Senator Carter Glass summed up his despair by exclaiming: "Why, if the President asked Congress to commit suicide tomorrow, they'd do it."

The impact on the justices varied. Roberts, the youngest among them and therefore not a direct target of the President's campaign, decided to resign if the measure were passed. Hughes, then 74, told his intimates, "If they want me to preside over a convention, I can do it." Brandeis, the eldest of the so-called Nine Old Men and one of the greatest liberals who ever sat on the Supreme Court bench, was cut to the quick by the President's indiscriminate assault upon age. Without exception, the justices were hostile to the scheme and resented the President's false inference that they were not able to keep up with their work.

The first jolt that the bill sustained was a wave of public reaction against the deceptive trappings of reform in which F. D. R. and Cummings had tried to camouflage their assault upon the court. Many, even among those who thought the conduct of the court had forced the President's hand, were critical of this indirection. It placed the Administration forces on the defensive from the very beginning.

A second severe jolt came when Senator Burton K. Wheeler read a letter from Chief Justice Hughes to the Senate Judiciary Committee, which was conducting hearings on the bill. Leaders of the fight in the Senate had asked the Chief Justice to appear in person, and he had agreed to do so if Justice Brandeis would accompany him. When he found that Brandeis believed strongly that no justice should testify in person, he contented himself with sending a letter setting forth the facts about the work of the court.

With cool logic, Hughes showed that the Supreme Court was fully abreast of its work, that it was very liberal in granting petitions for review, and that an increase in the size of the court would impair rather than enhance its efficiency. "There would be more judges to hear," he wrote, "more judges to confer, more judges to discuss, more judges to be convinced and to decide." Without touching on the major question of policy, Hughes left the President's arguments a shambles.

The Senate hearings produced a chorus of opposition to the bill from distinguished leaders in many walks of life. Such an outpouring of public opinion stiffened the spines of many legislators who had been worried but silent. The Republicans wisely kept in the background and let opponents of the bill in the President's own party lead the fight. The White House was increasingly alarmed by the disaffection of loyal New Dealers, but the President continued to scoff at any suggestion of compromise. To anxious members of his

CONTINUED ON PAGE 105

Last Survivors

In the misty memories of six centenarians

By THE REV. ELIAS

SAMUEL DOWNING

In the summer of 1864, as the Civil War dragged on, the Reverend Elias Brewster Hillard, a Congregational clergyman from Connecticut, was asked by a Hartford publisher to visit the last surviving soldiers of the American Revolution in order to record their memories of that earlier war and to obtain their views on "the present rebellion" imperiling the Union they had helped bring to birth.

Of all the men who had marched with Washington and Arnold, with Gates and Greene and Mad Anthony Wayne, only seven were still alive. All were past 100; the eldest, Lemuel Cook, was 105. Four lived in New York State, one in Maine, and one in Ohio; the seventh, James Barham, lived somewhere in Missouri, but he did not reply to inquiries and Mr. Hillard was unable to find him. With the possible exception of the Reverend Daniel Waldo, who was related to the Adamses of Quincy and who had served as chaplain of the House of Representatives, none was famous. Once participants in great and stirring events, they were now forgotten old men living out their remaining years with sons or daughters. (Samuel Downing's son was 73, but his father still called him "Bub.")

Samuel Downing lives in the town of Edinburgh, Saratoga County, New York. His age is one hundred and two years. . . . The house of Mr. Downing, built by himself, (was) the first framed house in the town of Edinburgh, seventy years ago. . . . Mr. Downing is altogether the most vigorous in body and mind of the survivors. Indeed, judging from his bearing and conversation, you would not take him to be over seventy years of age. His eye is indeed dim, but all his other faculties are unimpaired, and his natural force is not at all abated. Still he is strong, hearty, enthusiastic, cheery: the most sociable of men and the very best of company. Seated in the house, and my errand made known to him, he entered upon the story of his life, which I will give as nearly as possible in the old man's own words.

"I was born," said he, "in the town of Newburyport, Mass., on the 30th of November, 1761. . . . Well, the war broke out. They was enlisting three years men and for-the-war men. I heard say that Hopkinton was the enlisting place. I waited till dinner time, when I thought nobody would see me, and then I started. It was eighteen miles, and I went it pretty quick. The recruiting officer, when I told him what I'd come for, said I was too small. I told him just what I'd done. 'Well,' said he, 'you stay here and I'll give you a letter to Col. Fifield over in Charlestown and perhaps he'll take you.' So I staid with him; and when uncle and aunt came home that night they had no Sam. The next day I went and carried the letter to Col. Fifield, and he accepted me. But he wasn't quite ready to go: he had his haying to do; so I staid with him and helped him through it, and then I started for the war.

"The first duty I ever did was to guard wagons from

of the Revolution

recorded in 1864, the great war lives again

BREWSTER HILLARD

The minister was preceded in his tour by a photographer-artist who took the veterans' pictures and made sketches of their homes. Before Mr. Hillard set out on his own journey one of his subjects, Adam Link, died, and Mr. Hillard arrived at the home of the Reverend Daniel Waldo to find him on his deathbed. But Mr. Hillard obtained their stories from the photographer or from relatives and included them with the others in a slender yet moving book published that same year. Excerpts from it, including a photograph of each veteran and a sketch of his house, appear on these and the next four pages. The editors are indebted to Mr. Hillard's grandson, the poet Archibald MacLeish, who first brought this old book to their attention some years ago.

Within a very short time all these men would be dead and the country's last living link with its origins severed. But for a moment, in their own words and in Mr. Hillard's unobtrusive but perceptive descriptions, the six centenarians, "comrades in the old common conflict, take each other by the hand, and look into each other's faces, and tell to one another the story of their lives, before they say the last farewell."

Downing built this house in Edinburgh, New York

Exeter to Springfield. We played the British a trick; I can remember what I said as well as can be. We all started off on a run, and as I couldn't see anything, I said, 'I don't see what the devil we're running after or running away from; for I can't see anything.' One of the officers behind me said, 'Run, you little dog, or I'll spontoon you.' 'Well,' I answered, 'I guess I can run as fast as you can and as far.' Pretty soon I found they were going to surprise a British train. We captured it; and among the stores were some hogsheads of rum. So when we got back to camp that night the officers had a great time drinking and gambling; but none for the poor soldiers. Says one of the sergeants to me, 'We'll have some of that rum.' It fell to my lot to be on sentry that night; so I couldn't let 'em in at the door. But they waited till the officers got boozy; then they went in at the windows and drew a

pailful, and brought it out and we filled our canteens, and then they went in and drew another. So we had some of the rum; all we wanted was to live with the officers, not any better.

"Afterwards we were stationed in the Mohawk valley. Arnold was our fighting general, and a bloody fellow he was. He didn't care for nothing; he'd ride right in. It was 'Come on, boys!' 'twasn't 'Go, boys!' He was as brave a man as ever lived. He was dark-skinned, with black hair, of middling height. There wasn't any waste timber on him. He was a stern looking man, but kind to his soldiers. They didn't treat him right; he ought to have had Burgoyne's sword. But he ought to have been true. We had true men then; 'twasn't as it is now. Everybody was true: the tories we'd killed or driven to Canada."

"You don't believe, then, in letting men stay at

their homes and help the enemy?"

"Not by a grand sight!" was his emphatic reply. "The men that caught Andre were true. He wanted to get away, offered them everything. Washington hated to hang him; he cried, they said."

The student of American history will remember the important part which Arnold performed in the battle connected with the surrender of Burgoyne. Mr. Downing was engaged.

"We heard," he said, "Burgoyne was coming. The tories began to feel triumphant. One of them came in one morning and said to his wife, 'Ty (Ticonderoga) is taken, my dear.' But they soon changed their tune. The first day at Bemis Heights both claimed the victory. But by and by we got Burgoyne where we wanted him, and he gave up. He saw there was no use in fighting it out. There's where I call 'em *gentlemen*. Bless your body, we had *gentlemen* to fight with in those days. When they was whipped they gave up. It isn't so now.

"Gates was an 'old granny' looking fellow. When Burgoyne came up to surrender his sword, he said to Gates, 'Are you a general? You look more like a granny than you do like a general.' 'I be a granny,' said Gates, 'and I've delivered you of ten thousand men to-day.'

"By and by they began to talk about going to take New York. There's always policy, you know, in war. We made the British think we were coming to take the city. We drew up in line of battle: the British drew up over there (pointing with his hand). They looked very handsome. But Washington went south to Yorktown. LaFayette laid down the white sticks, and we threw up entrenchments by them. We were right opposite Washington's headquarters. I saw him every day."

"Was he as fine a looking man as he is reported to have been?"

"Oh!" he exclaimed, lifting up both his hands and pausing, "but you never got a smile out of him. He was a nice man. We loved him. They'd sell their lives for him." I asked, "What do you think he would say if he was here now?"

"Say!" exclaimed he, "I don't know, but he'd be mad to see me sitting here. I tell 'em if they'll give me a horse I'll go as it is. If the rebels come here, I shall sartingly take my gun. I can see best furtherest off."

"How would Washington treat traitors if he caught them?"

"Hang 'em to the first tree!" was his reply. . . .

"When peace was declared," said the old man, concluding his story of the war, "we burnt thirteen candles in every hut, one for each State."

ADAM LINK

Since [Adam Link's] picture was taken, he has passed away. He was born in Washington county, near Hagerstown, Maryland, November 14, 1761. He died at Sulphur Springs, Crawford county, Ohio, August 15, 1864. His age was one hundred and two.

The circumstances of Mr. Link's life were humble, and his part in the war unimportant. He enlisted at the age of sixteen, in Wheeling, Virginia, for the frontier service, and spent five years in that service, mostly in the vicinity of Wheeling. . . .

At the age of twenty-eight years, he married Elizabeth Link, a distant relative. After this, being fond of change, he roamed about from place to place. At the age of sixty, he walked one hundred and forty-one miles from his home in Pennsylvania to Ohio, accomplishing it in three days. When seventy years of age, he set about clearing a farm . . .

Perpetuating the habits of the frontier service, Mr. Link roughed it through life. His constitution must have been of iron to have endured his irregularities and excesses. He paid no attention to his manner of eating, and he was addicted to strong drink. Notwithstanding all, his health was good till near the very close of his life. . . . Upon the artist [when he took his photograph] telling him that he had come a long way to see him, he replied, "You can see me cheap now. Whatever else they may say of me, no man ever could call me a coward."

ALEXANDER MILLINER

At Adam's Basin, on the Rochester and Niagara Falls division of the Central Railroad, lives Alexander Milliner. Mr. Milliner was born at Quebec on the 14th of March, 1760. . . . On the 14th of March, of the present year, therefore, Mr. Milliner was one hundred and four years old. . . .

Too young at the time of his enlistment for service in the ranks, he was enlisted as drummer boy; and in this capacity he served four years, in Washington's Life Guard. He was a great favorite, he says, with the Commander-in-Chief. . . . His recollection of Washington is distinct and vivid: "He was a good man, a beautiful man. He was always pleasant; never changed countenance, but wore the same in defeat and retreat as in victory." Lady Washington, too, he recollects, on her visits to the camp. "She was a short, thick woman; very pleasant and kind. She used to visit the hospitals, was kind-hearted, and had a motherly care."

"One day," he continued, "the General sent for me to come up to headquarters, and told me to play. So I

took the drum, overhauled her, braced her up, and played a tune. The General put his hand in his pocket and gave me three dollars; then one and another gave me more—so I made out well; in all, I got fifteen dollars. I was glad of it: my mother wanted some tea, and I got the poor old woman some." His mother accompanied the army as washerwoman, to be near her boy.

He relates the following anecdote of General Washington: "We were going along one day, slow march, and came to where the boys were jerking stones. 'Halt!' came the command. 'Now, boys,' said the General, 'I will show you how to jerk a stone.' He beat 'em all. He smiled, but didn't laugh out."

Mr. Milliner was at the battles of White Plains, Brandywine, Saratoga, Monmouth, Yorktown, and some others. The first of these he describes as "a nasty battle." At Monmouth, he received a flesh wound in his thigh. "One of the officers came along, and, looking at me, said, 'What's the matter with you, boy?' 'Nothing,' I answered. 'Poor fellow,' exclaimed he, 'you are bleeding to death.' I looked down; the blood was gushing out of me. . . ."

Of Burgoyne's surrender he says, "The British soldiers looked down-hearted. When the order came to 'ground arms,' one of them exclaimed, with an oath, 'You are not going to have my gun!' and threw it violently on the ground, and smashed it. Arnold was a smart man; they didn't sarve him quite straight."

He was at the encampment at Valley Forge. "Lady Washington visited the army. She used thorns instead of pins on her clothes. The poor soldiers had bloody feet." At Yorktown he shook hands with Cornwallis. He describes him as "a fine looking man; very mild. The day after the surrender, the Life Guard came up. Cornwallis sat on an old bench. 'Halt!' he ordered; then looked at us—viewed us."

In all, Mr. Milliner served six years and a half in the army. Besides his service in the army, Mr. Milliner has served his country five years and a half in the navy. Three years of this service was on board the old frigate *Constitution*, he being in the action of February 20, 1814, in which she engaged the two British ships, the *Cyane* and the *Levant*, capturing them both. While following the sea he was captured by the French and carried into Guadaloupe. As a prisoner there, he suffered hard treatment. Of the bread which he says he has eaten in seven kingdoms, he pronounces that in the French prison decidedly the worst. . . .

At the time his photograph was taken he could still handle his drum, playing for the artist, with excellent time and flourishes which showed him to have been a master of the art. . . . His sight is as good yet as when young. He reads his Bible every day without the aid of glasses. His memory is clear respecting events which occurred eighty or ninety years ago. . . .

In the present conflict with treason, Mr. Milliner's sympathies, as with all his surviving Revolutionary comrades, are enlisted most strongly on the side of the Union; he declaring that it is "too bad that this country, so hardly got, should be destroyed by its own people."

DANIEL WALDO

WILLIAM HUTCHINGS

Syracuse, N.Y., was the home of Rev. Daniel Waldo. . . . Most painful was my disappointment on reaching his house to find that death was dealing with the old man. . . . His age was one hundred and one.

Daniel Waldo was born in Windham, (Scotland Parish), Conn., on the 10th of September, 1762. . . . In 1778, being then sixteen years old, he enlisted for eight months in the service of the State; and during the term of this enlistment, in March, 1779, was taken prisoner by the tories at Horseneck. One of the guards, on leaving his beat one stormy night, failed to give him warning, and thus the tories surprised him. One of them snapped a musket at him, but it only flashed in the pan; whereupon Mr. Waldo surrendered. This terminated his immediate connection with the war. Upon his release by exchange, he returned to his home, in Windham.

At the age of about twenty, becoming hopefully a Christian, he resolved to devote himself to the ministry . . . and for more than seventy years he was a minister in the Congregational Church. . . . In 1805, Mrs. Waldo became insane, and died seven years ago. "I lived," said the old man, in speaking of it, "fifty years with a crazy wife."

On the 22d of December, 1856, Mr. Waldo was chosen chaplain of the House of Representatives. He spent most of his time in reading, which he greatly loved—not wishing, as he used to say, to hear "the quarrels in the House."

William Hutchings was born in York, York county, Maine (then Massachusetts), in 1764. He is, therefore, in his one hundred and first year.

Mr. Hutchings' connection with the war of the Revolution was but limited. He enlisted at the age of fifteen for the coast defense of his own state; and this was the only service in which he was engaged during the war. The only fighting which he saw was at the siege of Castine, where he was taken prisoner; but the British, declaring it a shame to hold as prisoner one so young, promptly released him. . . .

The father of Mr. Hutchings had . . . in 1768 removed with his family from York to Penobscot, being one of the earliest settlers there. . . . They were finally beginning to live comfortably when the British took possession of the neighboring town of Castine, and drove his father from his home, who fled with his family to Newcastle, where he abode till the close of the war, while William remained to fight the foe. . . . Mr. Hutchings has been throughout life an early riser and a hard worker; not particularly regular in his habits. He smokes regularly, and uses spirituous liquors moderately. His mind is still vigorous, though his body is feeble. He is deeply interested in the present conflict. Speaking of General Grant and his prospects of success in his campaign against Richmond, he concluded by saying, "Well, I know two old folks up here in Maine who are praying for him."

LEMUEL COOK

Lemuel Cook is the oldest survivor of the Revolution. He lives in the town of Clarendon (near Rochester), Orleans county, New York. His age is one hundred and five years.

Mr. Cook was born in Northbury, Litchfield county, Connecticut, September 10, 1759. He enlisted at Cheshire, in that state, when only sixteen years old, served through the war, and was discharged in Danbury, June 12, 1784. The circumstances of his service he relates as follows:

"The first time I smelt gunpowder was at Valentine's Hill (West Chester, New York). A troop of British horse were coming. 'Mount your horses in a minute,' cried the colonel. I was on mine as quick as a squirrel. There were two fires—crash! Up came Darrow, good old soul! and said, 'Lem, what do you think of gunpowder? Smell good to you?'

"The first time I was ordered on sentry was at Dobbs' Ferry. A man came out of a barn and leveled his piece and fired. I felt the wind of the ball. A soldier near me said, 'Lem, they mean you; go on the other side of the road.' So I went over; and pretty soon another man came out of the barn and aimed and fired. He didn't come near me. Soon another came out and fired. His ball lodged in my hat. By this time the firing had roused the camp, and a company of our troops came on one side, and a party of the French on the other; and they took the men in the barn prisoners, and brought them in. This was the first time I saw the French in operation. They stepped as though on edge. They were a dreadful proud nation. When they brought the men in, one of them . . . told how they had each laid out a crown, and agreed that the one who brought me down should have the three. When he got through with his story, I stepped to my holster and took out my pistol, and walked up to him and said, 'If I've been a mark to you for money, I'll take my turn now. So, deliver your money, or your life!' He handed over four crowns, and I got three more from the other two."

Mr. Cook was at the battle of Brandywine and at Cornwallis' surrender. Of the latter he gives the following account: "It was reported Washington was going to storm New York. . . . Baron Steuben was mustermaster. He had us called out to select men and horses fit for service. When he came to me, he said, 'Young man, how old are you?' I told him. 'Be on the ground to-morrow morning at nine o'clock,' said he. . . . We marched off towards White Plains. Then 'left wheel,' and struck right north. Got to King's Ferry, below Tarrytown. There were boats, scows, &c. We went right across into the Jerseys. . . . Then we were in Virginia. There wasn't much fighting. Cornwallis tried to force his way north to New York; but fell into the arms of LaFayette, and he drove him back. We were on a kind of side hill. We had plaguey little to eat and nothing to drink under heaven. We hove up some brush to keep the flies off. Washington ordered that there should be no laughing at the British; said it was bad enough to have to surrender without being insulted. The army were paraded on a great smooth lot, and there they stacked their arms. Then came the devil—old women, and all (camp followers). One said, 'I wonder if the d—d Yankees will give me any bread.' The horses were starved out. Washington turned out with his horses and helped 'em up the hill. When they see the artillery, they said, 'There, them's the very artillery that belonged to Burgoyne.' Greene come from the southard: the awfullest set you ever see. Some, I should presume, had a pint of lice on 'em. No boots nor shoes."

The old man's talk is very broken and fragmentary. He recalls the past slowly, and with difficulty; his articulation, also, is very imperfect; but when he has fixed his mind upon it, all seems to come up clear. . . . He has voted the Democratic ticket since the organization of the government, supposing that it still represents the same party that it did in Jefferson's time. The old man's health is comfortably good. Altogether, he is a noble old man; and long may it yet be before his name shall be missed from the roll of his country's deliverers.

Young Samuel Slater smuggled a cotton mill out of England—in his head—

and helped start America's Industrial Revolution

FATHER *of our* FACTORY

Samuel Slater

Feats of memory, particularly of the kind of memory derided as "photographic"—for all the cornucopias of wealth they sometimes pour over television contestants—are looked down on in modern times, but they have their role in history. Consider, for example, the story of Samuel Slater. It would be impolite to call him a spy, for he would not have considered himself one. Furthermore, he was a man of peace. Yet in his own time this cotton spinner's apprentice achieved with his prodigious memory an effect as great as or greater than any successful military espionage has brought about in our own. For he successfully transplanted the infant Industrial Revolution, which was in many ways an English monopoly, across an ocean to a new country.

To understand Slater's feat, one must look back to the economic situation of England and America in the days directly after the Colonies had achieved their independence. If Britain no longer ruled her former colonies, she clung tenaciously to her trade with them. Thanks to her flourishing new textile industry, she was able to sell large quantities of cotton goods in the United States at prices so low there was little incentive left for making cloth over here by the old-fashioned hand methods. To maintain this favorable dependency as long as possible, England went to fantastic lengths to guard the secrets that had mechanized her cotton industry, and so effective were these measures that America might well have continued solely as an agricultural nation for years, had it not been for Samuel Slater.

Slater's first mill: In the tall building at the river's edge, once a fuller's mill, he designed from memory intricate machines like a 48-spindle Arkwright spinning frame (right).

SYSTEM

By ARNOLD WELLES

Slater was born near the town of Belper, in Derbyshire, and served his apprenticeship in Jedediah Strutt's cotton mills (foreground).

Slater was born in 1768 on his family's property, Holly House, in Derbyshire, England. His father, William Slater, was an educated, independent farmer and timber merchant, the close friend and neighbor of Jedediah Strutt, successively farmer, textile manufacturer, and partner of England's famous inventor, Sir Richard Arkwright, whose spinning frame had revolutionized the manufacture of cotton yarn. Three years after Samuel Slater's birth, Strutt had financed Arkwright's factory at Cromford—the world's earliest authentic cotton mill—where water power replaced humans and animals in moving the machinery, and where the whole operation of spinning yarn could be accomplished for the first time automatically under one roof. Within five years Arkwright's mills were employing over 5,000 workers, and England's factory system was launched.

It was in this atmosphere of industrial revolution that young Slater grew up. He showed signs of his future mechanical bent at a tender age by making himself a polished steel spindle with which to help wind worsted for his mother, and whenever he had the chance, he would walk over to nearby Cromford or Belper on the Derwent River to see the cotton mills which Strutt and Arkwright owned. In 1782 Strutt began to erect a large hosiery factory at Milford, a mile from the Slater property, and he asked William Slater's permission to engage his eldest son as clerk. Slater, who had noticed the ability and inclinations of his younger son, Samuel, recommended him instead, observing that he not only "wrote well and was good at figures" but was also of a decided mechanical bent.

Thus, at the age of fourteen, Samuel Slater went to

live and work with Strutt. When William Slater died shortly afterward, in 1783, young Samuel Slater signed his own indenture to learn cotton spinning as an apprentice in Strutt's factory until the age of 21.

During the early days of his term the boy became so engrossed in the business that he would go for six months without seeing his family, despite the fact that they lived only a mile away, and he would frequently spend his only free day, Sunday, experimenting alone on machinery. In those days millowners had to build all their own machinery, and Slater acquired valuable experience in its design, as well as its operation, and in the processes of spinning yarn. Even before completing his term of indenture he was made superintendent of Strutt's new hosiery mill.

But Slater had become concerned about the chances for an independent career in England. Arkwright's patents having expired, factories had sprung up everywhere, and Slater could see that to launch out on his own he would need more and more capital to stay ahead of the technical improvements constantly taking place. His attention had been drawn to the United States by an article in a Philadelphia paper saying that a bounty of £100 had been granted by the Pennsylvania legislature to a man who had designed a textile machine. Young Slater made up his mind that he would go to the United States and introduce the Arkwright methods there. As his first step, even before his term with Strutt expired, Slater obtained his employer's permission to supervise the erection of the new cotton works Arkwright was then starting, and from this experience he gained valuable knowledge for the future.

There were, it was true, grave risks to consider. Britain still strictly forbade the export of textile machinery or the designs for it. With France entering a period of revolution which might unsettle the economy of the Old World, it was even more important that the large American market be safeguarded for British commerce. As a result, the Arkwright machines and techniques were nowhere in use in America at the time, and various attempts—in Pennsylvania, Massachusetts, Connecticut, Maryland, and South Carolina—to produce satisfactory cotton textiles had borne little fruit. Without Arkwright's inventions it was impossible to make cotton yarn strong enough for the warps needed in hand-loom weaving.

Enterprising Yankees undertook all kinds of ingenious attempts to smuggle out modern machines or drawings. Even the American minister to France was involved in some of them: machinery would be quietly purchased in England, dismantled, and sent in pieces to our Paris legation for transshipment to the United States in boxes labeled "glassware" or "farm implements." British agents and the Royal Navy managed to intercept almost all such shipments, however, and skilled workers who attempted to slip away with drawings or models were apprehended on the high seas and brought back. Passengers leaving England for American ports were thoroughly searched by customs agents before boarding ship.

Slater knew of these handicaps and determined to take along nothing in writing save his indenture papers. Even these he was careful to conceal. As the time of his departure drew near he did not reveal his plans even to his family, telling his mother only that he was taking a trip to London. On September 1, 1789, in the warm sunlight of late summer, he cast one last look at the pleasant meadows and orchards of Holly House and set off through the lovely Derbyshire countryside.

In London he decided to spend a few days sightseeing, inasmuch as this was to be his first and last visit to the capital. Then, after posting a letter home revealing his intended journey, he boarded ship for New York, assuming the guise of a farmer to escape detection. The role was not difficult for the son of a Derbyshire yeoman, and except for the hidden indenture there was nothing to link the young man with the cotton textile industry. But he was carrying with him in a very remarkable memory the complete details of a modern cotton mill.

After a passage of 66 days, Slater's ship reached New York. He had originally intended to go to Philadelphia, but when he learned of the existence of the New York Manufacturing Company on Vesey Street in downtown Manhattan, he showed his indenture and got a job there instead. The company had recently been organized to make yarns and cloth, but the yarn was linen and the machinery, hand-operated, was copied from antiquated English models. This was a far cry from the factories Slater had supervised in Derbyshire, and he was unimpressed.

Fortunately, about this time, the newcomer happened to meet the captain of a packet sailing between New York and Providence, Rhode Island, and from him learned of the interest in textile manufacturing shown by a wealthy, retired merchant of Providence, Moses Brown, later to become one of the founders of Brown University. A converted Quaker and a man of large imagination and business acumen, Brown had invested considerable cash in two rough, hand-operated spinning frames and a crude carding machine as well as in a couple of obsolete "jennies." But all his attempts to produce cotton yarns had ended in failure, and he could find little use for his expensive machinery. Such was the situation when he received a letter from Slater:

New York, December 2d, 1789

SIR,—

A few days ago I was informed that you wanted a manager of *cotton spinning,* etc., in which business I flatter myself that I can give the greatest satisfaction, in making machinery, making good yarn, either for *stockings* or *twist.* as any that is made in England; as I have had opportunity, and an oversight of Sir Richard Arkwright's works, and in Mr. Strutt's mill upwards of eight years. If you are not provided for, should be glad to serve you; though I am in the New York manufactory, and have been for three weeks since I arrived from England. But we have but *one card, two machines,* two spinning jennies, which I think are not worth using. My *intention* is to erect a *perpetual card and spinning.* (Meaning the Arkwright patents). If you please to drop a line respecting the amount of encouragement you wish to give, by favor of Captain Brown, you will much oblige, sir, your most obedient humble servant.

SAMUEL SLATER

N.B.—Please to direct to me at No. 37, Golden Hill, New York.

Slater's letter fired the shrewd Quaker's imagination, and he hastened to reply, declaring that he and his associates were "destitute of a person acquainted with water-frame spinning" and offering Slater all the profits from successful operation of their machinery over and above interest on the capital invested and depreciation charges. His invitation concluded: "If the present situation does not come up to what thou wishes, and, from thy knowledge of the business, can be ascertained of the advantages of the mills, so as to induce thee to come and work ours, and have the *credit* as well as the advantage of perfecting the first water-mill in America, we should be glad to engage thy care so long as they can be made profitable to both, and we can agree."

RHODE ISLAND HISTORICAL SOCIETY

Moses Brown, a Quaker merchant, was Slater's financial backer.

37

These lithographs are from an unusual series called The Progress of Cotton, *published in the early nineteenth century, which shows all the steps in the processing of cotton from field to finished product. Three of the steps are illustrated here: at left, carded "ends," or*

Tempted and flattered, and assuming that the Providence operation needed only an experienced overseer to make it a success, Slater decided to accept. He took a boat in January, 1790, reached Providence on the eighteenth of the month, and immediately called on Moses Brown.

The two men were in striking contrast. Slater, only 21, was nearly six feet tall and powerfully built, with ruddy complexion and fair hair. Moses Brown, in his soft, broad-brimmed Quaker hat, was well past middle age, of small stature, with a pair of bright, bespectacled eyes set in a benevolent face framed by flowing gray locks. Satisfied from a glance at the Strutt indenture that his young caller was bona fide, Brown took Slater in a sleigh to the little hamlet of Pawtucket, a community consisting of a dozen or so cottages on both sides of the Blackstone River, just outside Providence. They stopped at a small clothier's shop on the river's bank, close by a bridge which linked Rhode Island and Massachusetts. Here was assembled Brown's ill-assorted machinery.

Slater took one look and shook his head, his disappointment obvious. Compared to Strutt's splendid mill this was almost a caricature. He spoke bluntly: "These will not do; they are good for nothing in their present condition, nor can they be made to answer." Brown urged him to reconsider, to give the machines

a try, but the young Englishman was not to be persuaded. At last, in desperation, the old merchant threw Slater a challenge:

"Thee said thee could make machinery. Why not do it?"

Reluctantly, Slater finally agreed to build a new mill, using such parts of the old as would answer, but only on one condition: that Brown provide a trusted mechanic to make the machinery which Slater would design and that the man be put under bond neither to disclose the nature of the work nor to copy it.

"If I don't make as good yarn as they do in England," Slater declared, "I will have nothing for my services, but will throw the whole of what I have attempted over the bridge!" Brown agreed, arranging in addition to pay Slater's living expenses.

Then the old merchant took his visitor to the cottage of Oziel Wilkinson, an ingenious ironmaster, with whom Slater could board. Wilkinson, also a Quaker, operated a small anchor forge using water power from the river, and there he turned out ships' chandlery, shovels, scythes, and other tools. As the young Englishman entered the Wilkinson home, his host's younger daughter shyly scampered out of sight, but Hannah, the elder, lingered in the doorway to look at the stranger. Slater fell in love with her. (Within two years they would be married, and Hannah Slater would later

"slivers," of cotton are fed from cylindrical cans into "drawing frames," which attenuate them
o produce more even slivers; the "mule" (center) stretches and spins the yarn and winds it
•n bobbins; in the "warp-winding" process (right) the yarn is attached to frames for weaving.

acquire fame in her own right as the discoverer of cotton sewing thread, which she first produced from the fine yarns her husband manufactured.) In the Wilkinson household young Slater found new parents who helped him overcome his homesickness and encouraged him in the first difficult months.

Part of that winter he spent experimenting with Moses Brown's crude carding machine, and he was able to improve the quality of cotton fleece it turned out. This, when spun by hand on the jennies, produced a better yarn, but one which was still too weak and uneven to be used as warp in the hand-weaving of cloth. Slater was downhearted; he realized that he must build everything from scratch.

The rest of the winter he spent assembling the necessary materials for constructing the Arkwright machines and processes. He lacked even the tools with which to make the complicated equipment, and he was forced to make many of them himself before any building could commence. Furthermore, without models to copy, he had to work out his own computations for all measurements. One of the most ingenious elements of the Arkwright inventions was the variation in speeds of various parts of the machines. Mathematical tables for these were not available anywhere save in England; Slater had to rely on his own extraor-

dinary memory. Nevertheless, by April, 1790, he was ready to sign a firm partnership agreement to build two carding machines, a drawing and roving frame, and two spinning frames, all to be run automatically by water power. He was to receive one dollar a day as wages, half-ownership in the machinery he built, and, in addition, one-half of the mill's net profits after it was in operation. Moses Brown had turned over the supervision of his textile investments to William Almy, his son-in-law, and Smith Brown, his cousin, and these two men became Slater's new partners.

Now, behind shuttered windows in the little clothier's building on the riverbank, young Slater began to design the first successful cotton mill in America. As he drew the plans with chalk on wood, Sylvanus Brown, an experienced local wheelwright, cut out the parts from sturdy oak and fastened them together with wooden dowels. Young David Wilkinson, Slater's future brother-in-law and like his father a skilled ironworker, forged shafts for the spindles, rollers for the frames, and teeth in the cards which Pliny Earle, of Leicester, Massachusetts, prepared for the carding machines. Before iron gearwheels and card rims could be made, Slater and Wilkinson had to go to Mansfield, Massachusetts, to find suitable castings. By autumn, working sixteen hours a day, Slater had more than fulfilled his agreement: he had built not two but three

CONTINUED ON PAGE 90

In John Blake White's famous painting Marion offers a British officer a meal of baked potatoes. Legend says that White had sat on Marion's knee as a child and remembered his features. The painting was reproduced on Confederate currency.

Fox

Around Francis Marion there has sprung up an overgrowth of legend as tangled as the swamps he fought in. Here is an authoritative account of his role in the Revolution

By GEORGE F. SCHEER

"Our band is few, but true and tried,
Our leader frank and bold;
The British soldier trembles
When Marion's name is told."

There is the poem, and there is the sentence or two in schoolbooks about the phantom general who sallied at night from his secret lair in the swamps to attack the British foe. And there is the sobriquet, the Swamp Fox. And that's about all anyone seems to remember about General Francis Marion—except, perhaps, that once he invited to dinner a British officer, in his camp under flag of truce, and served only fire-baked potatoes on a bark slab and a beverage of vinegar and water. "But, surely, general," the officer asked, "this cannot be your usual fare." "Indeed, sir, it is," Marion replied, "and we are fortunate on this occasion, entertaining company, to have more than our usual allowance." The visiting Briton is supposed to have been so impressed that he resigned his commission and returned to England, full of sympathy for the self-sacrificing American patriots. That's not exactly the way it happened, but no one has ever cared much about the details; that is the way it goes in the Marion legend, and it is the legend that Americans cherish.

That legend was the invention of a specialist in hero-making, and the story of its origin and growth is as remarkable as the story of the man it celebrates. It begins with one of Marion's devoted soldiers, Peter Horry, and it tells how he undertook, several years after Marion's death, to write a biography that would immortalize his old chief; how he discovered himself unequal to the task and gave it up; how, much later, his accidental partnership with the Reverend Mason Locke Weems resulted in the first life of General Marion, "a celebrated partizan officer in the Revolutionary War, against the British and Tories, in South Carolina and Georgia," drawn, according to the title page, "from documents furnished by his brother-in-arms, Brigadier General P. Horry," and by Marion's nephew; how that sensational little book, a captivating mélange of "popular heroism, religion, and morality," compounded of fact and much fiction, firmly established Francis Marion in the American imagination as the Robin Hood of the Revolution; and how, after that, post offices and towns and counties as far away as the Pacific Coast were named for him.

That first "biography" appeared in 1809, and the century and a half that has passed since its publication has done little to change the legendary portrait: the Marion of Parson Weems remains the Marion of American history. Yet when you piece together the surviving letters, the orderly books, the official reports, when you read the maps and go to the ground he fought over, you come to realize that Marion's daring forays and breathtaking adventures are not merely the romantic stuff of folk literature, but that they actually influenced the strategy of armies and made a definite and discernible contribution to the British defeat in the South.

Marion (mounted, second from left) *and his men, some of them swimming their horses, cross the Pee Dee on makeshift rafts. Few of his soldiers wore uniforms, and regular troops often laughed at their appearance.*

From the outbreak of the Revolution until the spring of 1780, Marion put in five useful, though relatively inactive, years as an officer of the Second South Carolina Continental Regiment. But it was as a relentless guerrilla who never let up on the British after they overran his state that he earned his significance in history. He was not the only partisan those hard times discovered, but he stayed in the field longer than any of the others and best understood and carried out the mission of the partisan. And, although he won no tide-turning battles, he had more than a little to do with what General Nathanael Greene, commanding the Southern Department, called "flushing the bird" that General Washington caught at Yorktown.

Marion was 48 at the time, "rather below the middle stature," one of his men recalled, "lean and swarthy. His body was well set, but his knees and ankles were badly formed. . . . He had a countenance remarkably steady; his nose was aquiline, his chin projecting; his forehead was large and high, and his eyes black and piercing." It was the kind of face some men considered "hard visaged."

He was a man with the steady habits of a modest planter who had lived alone most of his life. He ate and drank abstemiously; his voice was light but low when he talked, and that was seldom because he was not a talkative man.

In the field he wore a close, round-bodied, crimson jacket and the blue breeches piped in white of his old Continental regiment. His black leather hat was the hard, visored helmet of the Second South Carolina, adorned with a plume and, in front, a silver crescent engraved, "Liberty or death."

Whether he fought his brigade mounted or afoot—he usually rode to the enemy and then fought as infantry—he was always in the front of the attacks that made his name a terror in the British and Tory camp. But he was not given to ferocious gesture. In fact, they say he drew his sword, a light dress weapon, so seldom that it rusted in its scabbard. It was not for personal conspicuousness in battle that his men remembered him, but for a quiet fearlessness, for sagacity and perseverance, and for never foolishly risking himself or the brigade. They rode with confidence behind a man who never hesitated in the face of impossible odds to fight and run to live and fight another day. And he endeared himself to them when he slept with them on the ground, ate their fare, and endured fatigue and danger with the hardiest of them. They told, for example, that one night while he slept by the fire his helmet was scorched and his blanket half burned before he awoke. He smothered the flames, refused a blanket from any of them, and in the charred remains of his own slept out the night. For months afterward,

42

he weathered the nights uncomplainingly under his tattered blanket and rode through sun and shower with the shriveled helmet perched jauntily on his head.

Marion's men actually had no official status. They were purely volunteers. When they came into the field, their state was overrun by the British and their rebel government had evaporated. Of their own will they took up arms to fight the invader, and it was impossible to preserve any more discipline and regularity among them than their patriotism and the dangers of the moment imposed on them. Fighting without pay, clothing, or provisions furnished by a government, compelled to care for their families as well as to provide for their own wants, they were likely to go home at planting or harvest time, or whenever family needs became acute, or simply when the going got too dreary. Therefore, brigade strength fluctuated from as few as twenty or thirty men to as many as several hundred, and Marion had to plan his operations accordingly. He seldom could count on more than 150 to 200 men, and at least once he became so disgusted with their casual coming and going that he considered giving up his command and going to Philadelphia to seek a Continental Army appointment.

It was the constant charge by Marion's enemies that it was not patriotism but the appeal of plunder that held his men together. But the fact is Marion never allowed them to act as freebooters. The record of his orders and punishments is there in his orderly books. He made himself very clear: "Any soldier of any denomination who is found taking any article from any plantation either from white or black will be deemed a marauder & plunderer & shall suffer immediate death."

Despite their irregularities and occasional lapses, when Marion came to disband his men in December, 1782, he could say with complete sincerity, "The general returns his warmest thanks to the officers and men who with unwavered patience and fortitude have undergone the greatest fatigues and hardships and with a spirit and bravery which must ever reflect the highest honor on them. No citizens in the world have ever done more than they have." It was true of them. And it was true of him.

Marion was born in the country he defended to a second-generation French Huguenot family on the Cooper River in South Carolina. As a boy he lived in the vicinity of Georgetown, where he hunted and fished the salt marshes and inland swamps and semi-tropical woods. When he was 23 and his father, an unsuccessful planter, died, he and his mother and a brother settled for a time in upper St. John's, Berkeley. The tradition is that he served in a mounted troop on a bootless expedition to the Cherokee country in the first flare-up of the French and Indian War on the Carolina frontier. Two years later, as a light infantry lieutenant in Grant's 1761 campaign against the Cherokee, he won the praise of his commanding officer as an "active, brave, and hardy soldier; and an excellent partisan officer."

Shortly before the Revolution he acquired a place of his own on the Santee River and was just getting his bachelor house in order when war came. He was elected a captain of the Second South Carolina Regiment, steadily rose in Continental rank, served in the defense of Fort Sullivan in 1776 and the assault on Savannah in 1779, and for a time was in field command of the southern army when it wintered near the Georgia border. Through peaceful garrison times and stormy, he shared every fortune of his regiment except its last: when General Benjamin Lincoln surrendered his entire army, including the Second South Carolina, to Sir Henry Clinton at Charleston on May 12, 1780, Marion was not among the nearly 5,500 men who capitulated. For the last several weeks before the fall of the city he had been convalescing at home from an ankle injury.

With Lincoln's surrender, the worst disaster the Americans had suffered in all the war, the American cause both north and south seemed all but lost. In the North, Washington's worn-out army lay deteriorating in New Jersey. The French, upon whom he had relied for reinforcements, were bottled up by a British fleet at Newport. And an enfeebled Congress and an apathetic people were allowing their rebellion to expire from sheer exhaustion. In the South Georgia had already been occupied by the British since the winter of 1779, and within three weeks after Lincoln's surrender South Carolina appeared to be totally subjugated. Without firing a shot, British garrisons occupied a chain of posts commanding the interior from Augusta on the Savannah River and Ninety-Six on the Carolina frontier, northward to Rocky Mount, Hanging Rock, and Camden, and eastward to Cheraw and Georgetown on the coast.

But to the enemy's surprise and consternation, the paralysis that at first seized the South Carolinians was short-lived. Lord Charles Cornwallis, left by Clinton in command at Charleston when the commander in chief returned to New York, had hardly reported "everything wearing the face of tranquility and submission" when patriot guerrillas, seeming to spring from nowhere, began a fierce, harassing warfare against the conqueror, intercepting his supply trains, severing his communications, smashing British and Tory detached units.

The partisans took some encouragement from reports that a small, new Continental army had arrived in North Carolina; around this nucleus the militia of Virginia and the Carolinas might build a force strong enough to stop the northward advance of the redcoats. In late July, when his ankle would carry him, Marion rode northward to join it with a little troop of neighbors and former army comrades who felt the British had violated the paroles they had given. According to a Continental officer, they were "distinguished by small black leather caps and the wretchedness of their attire; their number did not exceed twenty men and boys, some white, some black, and all mounted, but most of them miserably equipped." Nevertheless, General Horatio Gates, commanding the army, recognized the value of Marion's familiarity with the country and ordered Marion and "the Volunteers Horse of So Carolina" to "march with and attend" him as he advanced toward the enemy's key post at Camden.

While on the march, the Marion story has it, Gates received a request from Major John James for an officer to take command of a brigade he had raised among the Scotch-Irish of Williamsburg Township on the Black River. Gates promptly assigned Marion to the command with orders to use the brigade to seize the Santee River crossings behind Camden and cut off British communication with that post and its avenue of retreat to Charleston.

Marion took command of James's brigade on Lynche's Creek about the tenth of August, 1780, and his partisan career began. After two lightning attacks on strong Tory encampments in the neighborhood, he divided his seventy men and sent a party under his old friend, Major Peter Horry, east of Lenud's Ferry on the Santee to destroy all boats and cover the crossings, while he marched westward for Murray's Ferry. After coming down on a British guard there in the night of the twenty-third, scattering the redcoats and burning the ferry boats, he turned upriver toward Nelson's Ferry, 25 miles away.

Near dusk he picked up a British deserter who told him that Gates's army, upon reaching Camden, had been routed by the British on the sixteenth with incredible losses. From the deserter he also learned that a British escort with 150 Continental prisoners from Camden planned to rest that night at a house north of Nelson's Ferry. Without sharing with his men the depressing news of Gates's defeat, for fear they would desert him, he pushed his march all night and descended on the escort at dawn. Trapping many of the redcoats in the house, he killed two, wounded five, took twenty prisoners, and released the captured Continentals. But Marion's men heard from the prisoners that Gates had been defeated, and half of them slipped away within an hour. Marion, discovering that a heavy British patrol was in his rear, sent his prisoners toward North Carolina and retreated eastward toward the Pee Dee to make a junction with Major Horry's detachment.

Marion had no idea where the remnant of Gates's army was, or when or if it would ever be in "condition to act again." Colonel Thomas Sumter, who had bedeviled the enemy in the west, had been cut to pieces two days after the Camden debacle. Marion's little brigade was the only rebel force left intact in the state. With most of his men gone home, he now was forced, after a couple of brushes with enemy columns, to withdraw into North Carolina.

But within two weeks, he had heard from Gates at Hillsboro: North Carolina was aroused, the army was putting itself back together; in South Carolina Whig militia was assembling. Unfortunately, the Tories were gathering, too, and Gates would be pleased, he wrote, if Marion would advance to the Little Pee Dee River and disperse them. At the same time Marion heard from South Carolina that north of Georgetown the enemy had laid waste a path seventy miles long and fifteen wide as a punishment to the inhabitants who had "joined Marion and Horry in their late incursion"; the men who had left him at Nelson's Ferry were spoiling for revenge and ready to come out again. So on a Sunday evening, the twenty-fourth of September, with only thirty or forty men, Marion marched back into the heart of the enemy's northeasternmost defenses in South Carolina around Kingston.

The marches and actions that ensued between Marion and the British and Tories are hard to follow, even on large-scale maps of the river-and-swamp country of South Carolina, and they are almost lost in the larger history of the campaigns in the South; but they were shrewdly planned, smoothly executed, and very damaging to the enemy. To them Marion brought not only the training of an officer of the regular service and the remembered experience of Indian-style fighting on the frontier, but also an intimate knowledge of the country. And it was the terrain that gave to the native fighter a distinct advantage. It was unbelievably flat, unbelievably wet, and unbelievably wild—this world of the low country. North and south some eighty miles from Charleston and west some fifty were its roughly figured boundaries, and down across it swept seven large rivers and many smaller ones which gave it its character. For miles bordering them were the deep, vast, and gloomy cypress swamps. And between the great swamps were the forbidding shrub bogs, spongy tangles of impenetrable smilax, holly, myrtle, and jessamine, and broad brakes of cane. No roads crossed the swamps and bogs, except the secret paths of the hunter; only a few highroads, following the ridges between the great rivers and passing through forests of moss-hung live oak, tied together the plantations and scattered towns. Maps were not of much use off the main roads. But it was country that Marion knew and understood, so that for him its trails became avenues of swift surprise attack and safe retreat, its swamps and bogs his covert.

In this country during that fall of 1780, Marion's men fought at Black Mingo, northwest of Georgetown. It was another night attack, but their horses' hoofs clattering on a wooden bridge gave them away, so that they lost the element of surprise and learned ever after to lay down their blankets when crossing a bridge near the enemy. They raided Georgetown, but could not draw the garrison out of the town redoubt for a stand-up fight. Another night they pounced on Tory militia at Tarcote Swamp, near the forks of Black River.

It was of such incidents that Parson Weems made highly diverting tales. A friendly lad comes to camp to tell that tomorrow night "there is to be a mighty gathering of the tories" near his home, seventy miles away. "Having put our firearms in prime order for an attack, we mounted; and . . . dashed off, just as the broad-faced moon arose; and by daybreak next morning, had gained a very convenient swamp, within ten miles of the grand tory rendezvous. To avoid giving alarm, we struck into the swamp, and there, man and horse, lay snug all day. . . . Soon as it was dark, we mounted, and took the track at a sweeping gallop, which, by early supper time, brought us in sight of their fires. . . .

"Observing that they had three large fires, Marion divided our little party of sixty men into three companies, each opposite to a fire, then bidding us to take aim, with his pistol he gave the signal for a general discharge. In a moment the woods were all in a blaze, as by a flash of lightning, accompanied by a tremendous clap of thunder. Down tumbled the dead; off bolted the living; loud screamed the wounded; while far and wide, all over the woods, nothing was to be heard but the running of tories. . . .

"The consternation of the tories was so great that they never dreamt of carrying off anything. Even their fiddles and fiddle bows, and playing cards, were all left strewed around their fires.

"One of the gamblers, (it is a *serious truth*) though shot dead, still held the cards hard gripped in his hands. Led by curiosity to inspect this strange sight, a

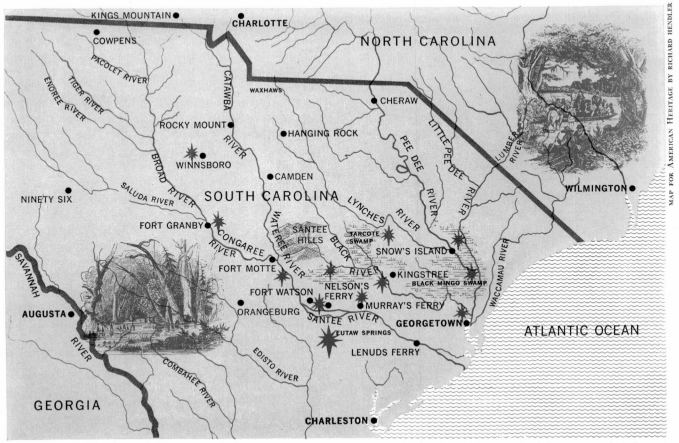

Marion's operations took place in a low, swampy region drained by many rivers. His major skirmishes are marked in red.

The dashing Marion, brandishing a saber, was the idol of his men. Historian Benson Lossing noted, "The followers of Robin Hood were never more devoted to their chief than were the men of Marion's brigade to their beloved leader."

dead gambler, we found that the cards which he held were ace, deuce, and jack. Clubs were trumps. Holding high, low, jack, and the game, in his own hand, he seemed to be in a fair way to do well; but Marion came down upon him with a trump that spoiled his sport, and non-suited him forever."

No wonder that the Parson captured the fancy of a young America!

They were small engagements, poorly chronicled, though poet-sung ("A moment in the British camp—a moment—and away, back to the pathless forest, before the peep of day."), but as the weeks passed into winter, Lord Cornwallis began to feel the cumulative effect of them. When Marion had retreated into North Carolina in September, Cornwallis had advanced toward Virginia as far north as Charlotte before his detached left wing had been destroyed by rebel frontiersmen at Kings Mountain and he had stumbled back sixty miles to Winnsboro to recover himself. In that hamlet,

northwest of Camden, he encamped for three miserable, wet months, October to January; and his letters from there make it reasonably clear that, although much of his strength had been lost at Kings Mountain and he had to await reinforcements from New York, it was the work of the partisans, especially of Marion, that tied him to Winnsboro and prevented his moving northward again. To his superior he reported: "Bad as the state of our affairs was on the northern frontier [around Ninety-Six, Rocky Mount, and Hanging Rock], the eastern part [on the vital Santee River line] was much worse. . . . Colonel Marion had so wrought on the minds of the people, partly by the terror of his threats and cruelty of his punishments, and partly by the promise of plunder, that there was scarcely an inhabitant between the Santee and Pee Dee that was not in arms against us. Some parties had even crossed the Santee and carried terror to the gates of Charleston."

Lieutenant Colonel Banastre Tarleton was even more specific: "Mr. Marion, by his zeal and abilities, showed himself capable of the trust committed to his charge. He collected his adherents at the shortest notice, in the neighborhood of Black River, and, after making incursions into the friendly districts, or threatening the communications, to avoid pursuit, he disbanded his followers. The alarms occasioned by these insurrections frequently retarded supplies on their way to the army; and a late report of Marion's strength delayed the junction of the recruits, who had arrived [in Charleston] from New York for the corps in the country."

The one man Cornwallis thought capable of running down and destroying the elusive Marion was Tarleton himself. In South Carolina, after his savage slaughter of Buford's troops at the Waxhaws, Tarleton was known as "the Butcher" and was without question the most bitterly hated of all the redcoats. In the British Army, where his loyalist legion was famed for its energy, prowess, and daring, he had risen swiftly and at 26 was regarded as perhaps the most valuable leader of mounted troops. "I therefore sent Tarleton," Cornwallis reported, "who pursued Marion for several days, obliged his corps to take to the swamps. . . ."

There was more to it than that. Marion led Tarleton a chase in that November of 1780. Tarleton was sixteen miles north of Nelson's Ferry when he discovered that Marion was a few miles south of him and struck out after him. About dark Marion cut through the Woodyard, a broad and tangled swamp, and camped for the night six miles beyond it. Tarleton dared not cross the Woodyard in the dark. As he was riding around it in the morning, Marion continued down Black River 35 miles "through woods and swamps and bogs, where there was no road." Tarleton, after making his way "for seven hours through swamps and defiles," hit 23 miles of fair road and then ran into Ox Swamp, where the chase went out of him.

Tradition has it that when Tarleton turned back (or was called off by a courier with orders to turn about and go after Sumter in the west) he gave Marion his sobriquet: "Come on, my boys, let's go back. As for this damned old fox, the devil himself could not catch him."

For all his pursuing, Tarleton merely gave exercise to Marion's brigade; for several more weeks the old fox was busily gnawing at British supply trains and posts and parties. Then, with his ammunition and supplies nearly exhausted, he took up an encampment in a romantic spot not far from the original ground of the Williamsburg men; it was called Snow's Island and was a large, high, river swamp plateau at the joining of Lynche's Creek with the Great Pee Dee. Here, deep in a forest of cypress, laurel, and pine, protected by the watercourses and tangles of canebrake and vines, he made a supply depot and rest camp that served him, off and on, for the rest of the war. From the island he threw into the lower country patrols which soon had Cornwallis complaining that they "keep the whole country in continual alarm, and render the assistance of regular troops everywhere necessary."

Through the rest of the winter of 1780 and into the spring of 1781, Marion played his partisan role while great events wrought great changes in the condition of the American cause in the South. In December General Nathanael Greene arrived at Charlotte to succeed Gates in command of the Continental Army of the Southern Department. By mid-April, 1781, in perhaps the most brilliant campaign of the war, he had maneuvered a greatly weakened and confused Cornwallis into Virginia and returned to South Carolina to battle for repossession of the state.

As Greene advanced toward Camden, Marion, joined by the splendid legion of young Light Horse Harry Lee, moved against the inner chain of British posts on the Santee and Congaree. Fort Watson, their first objective, was a tremendous, stockaded work crowning an ancient Indian mound that rose almost forty feet above the surrounding plain, north of Nelson's Ferry on the Santee. When Marion and Lee failed after a week to starve out the garrison by siege, they managed to effect a surrender by firing down on the fort from a log tower, devised by a country major of Marion's brigade who probably had never heard of the warring Romans.

By May 6 when they reached Fort Motte on the Congaree, Marion and Lee had a light fieldpiece,

ENGRAVING AFTER A PAINTING BY SIR JOSHUA REYNOLDS; CULVER SERVICE

Banastre Tarleton, Marion's pursuer, was described as "rather below the middle size, stout, strong, heavily made . . . his eyes small, black and piercing." He could also be ruthless. Marion complained, "He spares neither Whig nor Tory."

begged from Greene's army, but it did them no good. Fort Motte consisted of a strong stockade with outer trenches and an abatis built about a handsome brick mansion on a commanding piece of ground. They spent six days digging parallels and trenches and mounting their gun, but the fieldpiece failed to make a dent in the heavy timbers of the stockade or the walls of the house. Again the attackers resorted to primitive methods. Getting up close under cover of the siege lines, a man of Marion's brigade flung ignited pitch balls on the roof, set it afire, and smoked the enemy out. That night Mrs. Rebecca Motte, who had taken residence in her overseer's cottage when the British confiscated her house, entertained both the victors and the vanquished at what Colonel Lee called "a sumptuous dinner."

One by one the British posts fell. After repulsing Greene, the British evacuated Camden. Augusta surrendered, and Fort Granby. The British blew up their

CONTINUED ON PAGE 111

The sun set in a clear sky behind Charleston the afternoon of February 17, 1864. The besieged city lay in defiant silence, watching the Federal monitors at the entrance to the harbor. Out at Fort Sumter, where the war had begun, the faint boom of the sunset gun proclaimed that the little pile of rubble, now scarcely more than a symbol of resistance, was still held by its Confederate garrison. As the shadows lengthened, picket boats put out from the ironclads to begin the nightly vigils which the Federal Admiral John Dahlgren had so insistently prescribed.

Outside the bar, where the wooden ships comprising Dahlgren's second line of blockade lay guarding the harbor's entrance, the handsome sloop of war U.S.S. *Housatonic* prepared for a quiet night. A slight mist lay on the water as lookouts of the first watch took their stations. They were watchful but relaxed; it was not the sort of night a blockade-runner would choose for crossing the bar, and besides, the hard-driving Dahlgren was away on a trip to Port Royal.

About 8:45, Acting Master J. K. Crosby, officer of the deck, observed a slight disturbance in the water about a hundred yards distant and abeam. Crosby thought it was a porpoise, or a school of fish, or even a plank moving in the water. Whatever it was, it came on directly toward the ship. Crosby looked once more, decided to take no chances, and gave orders to slip the chain, beat to quarters, and call the captain.

His decision was a wise one. The *Housatonic* was about to experience the only submarine attack of the Civil War.

The *Housatonic*'s dubious distinction came about by chance. If David Farragut had waited longer to capture New Orleans, Acting Master Crosby would have stood an uneventful watch. For the story of the Confederate submarine *H. L. Hunley*, known variously and mistakenly as the *Fish*, the *American Diver*, and the *David*, and nicknamed with grim accuracy the Peripatetic Coffin, really began in New Orleans. But for the early fall of that city, the *Hunley*'s builders would never have begun a journey that led, eventually, to Charleston.

Sometime in 1861, James R. McClintock and Baxter Watson of New Orleans, marine engineers and machinists, determined to build a submarine at private expense and operate it against the Federal blockade at the mouth of the Mississippi.

No submarine in recorded history had ever sunk a ship in combat, but McClintock and Watson were not discouraged by this. David Bushnell's one-man submersible, the *Turtle*, had almost done the trick during the Revolutionary War, and Robert Fulton's later submarine demonstrations left no doubt that men of daring and ingenuity could make and operate a lethal undersea weapon. Caught up in the fervor of the war's first year, the two engineers determined to try.

To patriotism was added another motive, profit. At the start of the war, Jefferson Davis had invited ap-

An unknown Yankee based this drawing of the Hunley *on rumor. He put eleven men instead of eight on the shaft and failed to link it to the propeller.*

SUBMARINE LIBRARY

plications for letters of marque authorizing private citizens to wage war against Union vessels. The Confederate government was ready to pay handsome financial prizes for the destruction of enemy men-of-war. A submarine operated with any success in the waters of a blockaded port might pay its way and show a return on the investment without ever going to sea.

Work on the boat began late in 1861. As expenses mounted, others joined in the project—John K. Scott, Robin R. Barron, H. J. Leovy, and Horace L. Hunley, a man whose enthusiasm for submarines was to grow with every setback. In the spring of 1862 the submarine, christened the *Pioneer*, was ready for a trial run in Lake Pontchartrain. When she destroyed a target barge, the enthusiasm of her owners was boundless. A letter of marque was obtained and plans were laid for action against the blockade.

At this point, Farragut entered the picture. He moved up the Mississippi late in April and captured New Orleans. The *Pioneer* disappeared, sunk either by accident or design, and was forgotten until it was found and raised many years later. McClintock, Watson, and Hunley packed their bags and moved to Mobile.

Farragut would come to Mobile, too, but not until the summer of 1864. When the ardent trio of submarine builders from New Orleans arrived, the city seemed an ideal spot for their work. There were plenty of enemy vessels for their craft to operate against

when they built it; there were shops in Mobile and about as much raw material for the construction as could be found anywhere in the blockaded South; and the city was under the command of an imaginative officer, Major General Dabney H. Maury, who was sympathetic toward projects involving underwater torpedoes. He welcomed the three men heartily, approved their plans for private financing of the project, and ordered the boat to be built in the machine shops of Park & Lyons. Furthermore, he extended technical assistance. Two young engineers from the 21st Alabama Infantry, Lieutenants George E. Dixon and William A. Alexander—the latter an Englishman who had come to America in 1859—were detached for special duty at the shops.

A submarine was built and towed off Fort Morgan to be manned for an attack on the blockading fleet. It promptly sank, and the job had to be done all over again. It is with this third effort that we are concerned.

Somewhere an iron boiler was found, about twenty-five feet long and four feet in diameter, and the builders went to work to make a submarine out of it. They cut it in two longitudinally, tapered it fore and aft, inserted boiler-iron strips in the sides, and attached bow and stern castings. Inside the castings, bulkheads were riveted across to form water-ballast tanks for use in raising and lowering the boat. Of the tanks, Alexander noted later that "unfortunately these were left open on top"—a colossal understatement.

The Confederates' Hunley *was the first*

submarine to sink an enemy warship, but her

crude design made her a coffin for her crew

By LYDEL SIMS

A strip twelve inches wide was riveted the full length on top, and flat castings were fitted to the outside bottom for ballast, fastened by bolts which passed through stuffing boxes inside the boat so they might be loosened to drop the ballast if necessary. Sea cocks were installed in the water-ballast tanks, and force pumps to eject the water.

Propulsion was the big problem. Coal could not be burned below water, both because of the limited air supply and for lack of a smokestack. A storage battery adequate to operate even the smallest submarine had not yet been invented. The builders spent weeks trying to devise some kind of electromagnetic engine but finally gave it up and settled for manual power. A propeller shaft was installed almost the length of the boat, supported on the starboard side by brackets, with eight cranks spaced so that the crew could sit on the port side and turn the cranks. The arrangement left no room to pass fore and aft, but at least it assured some motion in the water.

For depth control another shaft was installed, pass-

Fore and aft on the boat's flat deck, hatchways were installed with coamings eight inches high. Glass panes installed in the coamings provided the only means of seeing out of the boat when the hatches were closed. There was no periscope. An air box was set between the hatchways and equipped with a pipe so that fresh air could be taken in on the surface without opening the hatches. All in all, it was a fantastically primitive affair.

The boat was boarded from both ends, part of the crew passing through the forward hatch with the skipper entering last, and the rest entering through the after hatch with the second officer in the rear. The seven crew members took their seats facing the propeller shaft, the two officers fastened down the hatch covers, and the skipper lit a candle which would provide illumination under water and also give warning when the oxygen supply ran low.

When all was ready, the first and second officers let water into the ballast tanks until the water level outside reached the glasses in the hatch coamings, an indication that the deck was about three inches under water. Then the sea cocks were closed, the second officer took his seat with the others at the propeller shaft, and the cranking began. The captain, still standing, lowered the fin lever and the boat slid deeper under the water, the mercury gauge indicating its depth. When he was ready to rise, he raised the lever, elevating the forward ends of the fins; as the boat reached its normal ballast trim of three inches below the surface, or earlier if the captain chose, he and the second officer operated the pumps to force water from the tanks, lightening the boat. When they were

PAINTING BY CONRAD WISE CHAPMAN, FROM THE CONFEDERATE MUSEUM

Guarded by a Rebel sentinel, the tiny Hunley *lies on a Charleston dock for overhaul about six weeks before the successful attack in which she went down for the last time.*

ing laterally through the boat just forward of the end of the propeller shaft. This controlled lateral fins, five feet long and eight inches wide, on the outside. A lever amidships allowed the fins to be raised or lowered. For the pilot's guidance, a mercury gauge was attached to the shell near the forward ballast tank to indicate the depth of the boat when submerged, and a compass was installed nearby. A wheel, acting on rods that ran the length of the boat, operated the rudder.

safely afloat and ready to land, the second officer opened his hatch cover, climbed out, and passed a line ashore.

She could go four miles an hour in smooth water and remain submerged as long as the air lasted. She was named the *H. L. Hunley,* in honor of her chief financial backer.

The torpedoes were copper cylinders holding charges of ninety pounds of explosive each, with percussion and friction primer mechanisms set off by flaring triggers. The plan for firing them was as desperate as everything else connected with the project. A torpedo attached to the submarine by a line two hundred feet long would float behind the boat, which would approach its prey, dive under it, and surface on the far side. The torpedo would thus be dragged against the target and explode.

Almost from the moment she was put into the water, the *Hunley* was plagued with trouble and disaster. Her first trial in the smooth waters of the Mobile River was a success; as General Maury watched, she towed a floating torpedo, dived under an old flatboat and scored a hit, blowing fragments a hundred feet into the air. But once she was taken out into the choppy waters of the bay, it was another story. She responded poorly, she was in constant danger of swamping, and that deadly torpedo trailing behind her was continually swinging in the direction of the wrong boat.

In later months, when the *Hunley*'s latent tendency to drown her crews had become virtually a fixed habit and she had become known as the Peripatetic Coffin, it was generally reported that she sank first in Mobile Bay, drowning a full crew of nine men. This is apparently incorrect; but though she did not sink until later, General Maury and her owners alike agreed that her future in Mobile Bay was exceedingly dubious.

They talked it over and decided Charleston would be a better base of operations. Nowhere was the need for aid more acute than at this beleaguered port in the summer of 1863. Fort Sumter was under almost constant bombardment, a combined land and sea attack was underway, and the magnificent Federal ironclad, the *New Ironsides,* loomed as one of the greatest threats to the city. If the *Hunley* could slip out some night and sink that great ship, it would be a tremendous blow for the Confederacy.

Maury, accordingly, offered the privately owned boat to General P. G. T. Beauregard, commander of the city's defenses. Beauregard had been trying in vain to establish a fleet of torpedo boats, but the big brass of the Confederate Navy had been slow to assist him. Why waste money on torpedo boats when you can build ironclads?

To Beauregard, the offer must have come almost as an answer to prayer. He accepted, the *Hunley* was loaded on two flatcars for what must have been one of the most remarkable railroad trips of the war, and destiny's date with the *Housatonic* drew nearer.

And now the *Hunley*'s difficulties began in earnest. Beauregard asked Commodore John R. Tucker, flag officer at Charleston, for naval volunteers to operate the deadly-looking little boat. Lieutenant John Payne, an Alabamian whose valor had been demonstrated in a skirmish with enemy pickets only a few weeks before, immediately asked for the command. A crew joined him, and the *Hunley* was towed to Fort Johnson for trial runs.

A few nights later tragedy struck. The submarine was lying at the wharf, ready to go out for a dive. The crew members had already taken their places, and Payne was standing forward ready to close the hatchway, when the swell from a passing steamer poured over the deck. The *Hunley* swamped and went down like a rock.

Payne escaped through the open hatch, watched the

The U.S.S. Housatonic *heels over as the* Hunley*'s torpedo strikes. She was floating in shallow water, and most of her crew survived by clinging to her masts and rigging.*

bubbles rising where the boat had sunk, and grimly asked permission to raise the boat, collect another crew, and try again.

The experiment might have been given up at this point except for an event that electrified Charleston, delighted Beauregard, and redoubled the optimism of the *Hunley*'s backers.

While the *Hunley* had been traveling across country on her flatcars, work was being completed at Charleston on a small iron boat that lay low in the water with

CONTINUED ON PAGE 107

THE LOVER'S LETTER BOX.

COMPOSED BY

W. T. WRIGHTON.

BOSTON.
Published by OLIVER DITSON & CO. 277 Washington St.

C.C. CLAPP & CO.   S.T. GORDON   BECK & LAWTON.   TRUAX & BALDWIN
Boston   N.York   Philad.a   Cinn.

MUSIC HAD CHARMS

Homely sentiment and crude humor—in delightful covers—

helped soothe the mid-nineteenth-century breast

I hear America singing," wrote Walt Whitman in 1860, and on a quantitative basis, at least, the air was as full of quavering voices, scraping fiddles, and tinkling pianos as—in other ways, in different rhythms—it is today. The publishers of the confection at the left, for example, advertised 33,000 different pieces of sheet music in 1867—most of them especially aimed at the family group around the parlor upright. In the days before radio and television and before we developed a special musical form in jazz, this kind of singing was widespread. It was homely and unsophisticated, filled with maidens' blushes and everyone's tears, with crude humor and sentiment, and with the same appeals to the headlines which characterize Tin Pan Alley today. And, not to put too fine a point on it, most of this outpouring was as bad as the popular music of our own time—if not a little worse. The era produced Stephen Foster, Dan Emmett, a few good hymns, and the music of the Civil War; but, in general, America had a tin ear.

What distinguishes the sheet music of a century ago, and spurs collectors on, is the vanished charm of its appearance. Song publishers discovered early that much of the selling power of their product depended on the attractiveness of the cover. Thus they came to work with some of the best lithographers in America at a time when the art of soft-stone engraving was at its peak. Most of the major engraving firms of the period—in particular, Nathaniel Currier, Sarony of New York, and J. H. Bufford of Boston—did song "fronts" at one time or other, and occasionally they hired struggling young artists like Alfred Jacob Miller and Winslow Homer. On the following pages some notable examples of the stone engraver's art are reproduced—and with them, for those who care to experiment, some less memorable examples of the songwriter's craft. All appear through the courtesy of Lester S. Levy of Baltimore, whose famous American music collection includes more than 25,000 song sheets.

When birds are singing in distress, and nature's face is fair,
Where wild flowers bring the busy bees I often wander there;
To meet young Harry in the grove; But where can Harry be!
I plac'd a letter to my love, in yonder hollow tree;
In yonder hollow tree, In yonder hollow tree,
I plac'd a letter to my love, in yonder hollow tree.

No "Postman's knock" or ringing bell, No maids to peep and see;
Dear Harry knows this very well, He's sure to come to me;
Young Cupid ever watches near, The lover's hollow tree;
He'll see me safe, I've nought to fear, While Harry's true to me;
Dear Harry's true to me, Dear Harry's true to me,
He'll see me safe, I've nought to fear, While Harry's true to me.

53

GENERAL TOM THUMB & LADY

GENERAL TOM THUMB'S
GRAND WEDDING MARCH

COMPOSED BY
E. MACK.

Philadelphia LEE & WALKER, 722 Chestnut St.

TO Mrs AMELIA BLOOMER.

THE NEW COSTUME POLKA
COMPOSED
FOR THE PIANO
by
MATHIAS KELLER.

Philadelphia, Lee & Walker, 162 Chesnut St.

SUCCESSORS TO GEO. WILLIG.

NEW YORK,   BALTIMORE, MD,   NEW ORLEANS
Mrs HALL & SON.   F. LEWIS.   MrT. T. MAYO

TO CYRUS W. FIELD, ESQ.

ATLANTIC TELE GRAPH POLKA.

THE NIAGARA & AGAMEMNON COMMENCING TO LAY THE CABLE.

COMPOSED BY A. TALEXY.

FULL SIZE AND APPEARANCE OF CABLE

MAP OF THE TELEGRAPH BETWEEN AMERICA & EUROPE.

BOSTON.
Published by OLIVER DITSON & CO 277 Washington St.

C. C. CLAPP & CO.   S. T. GORDON,   TRUAX & BALDWIN.
Boston.   N. York.   Phila.   Cinn.

TO Wm. F. CHASE.
OF SUFFOLK HOSE CO. No 5.
BOSTON.

HOMELESS TO NIGHT
OR
BOSTON
IN
ASHES

WORDS and
MUSIC BY
L. A. WHITE

BOSTON.
White, Smith & Perry.
298 & 300 Washington St.

The headlines, with disaster a specialty

"I Do Not Want To Be Drowned"
a song
Respectfully Dedicated to the Survivors of the Wreck of the
GOLDEN-GATE
Poetry by Frank Soule Esq. Music by P.R. Nicholls.
SAN FRANCISCO.
Printed & Published by Chas. F. Robbins & Co.

In a day when polkas, waltzes, and quadrilles were the rage of America, music publishers often found that they could push nondescript dance tunes by giving them topical lyrics and colorful "fronts." The four covers shown at left commemorate subjects as diverse as the 1863 marriage of two of P. T. Barnum's midgets, Tom Thumb and Lavinia Warren; Amelia Bloomer's innovations in feminine attire; the laying of the Atlantic Cable in 1858; and the great fire in downtown Boston in 1872.

In 1862 the steamship *Golden Gate* burned and sank off the west coast of Mexico. In appropriately heroic terms, the song at right described the rescue of a child from the wreck:

On deck there is terror and agony wild,
　"The ship is on fire!" is the ominous sound;
And pleading for life hear a motherless child,
　"Oh save me, do please, I don't want to be drowned!"

"Cling close to me, Addie!" a hero replied,
　"I'll risk my own life, little darling, for thee."
Then sprang with her over the ship's heated side,
　From merciless flames to the pitiless sea.

They're riding the wave, he is breasting the foam,
　She's clinging for life to the neck of the brave,
But over them rushes the breaker's high comb
　And Addie sinks under the ravenous wave.

Yet never despair for at mercy's command,
　The ocean its prey shall uninjured restore.
See! Addie is seized by a rescuing hand,
　And stands like a nymph on the desolate shore.

THE CHARMING YOUNG WIDOW I MET IN THE TRAIN

3. *The Widow and I side by side sat together*
The carriage containing ourselves and no more,
When silence was broken by my fair companion
Who enquired the time by the watch that I wore.
I of course satisfied her, and then conversation
Was freely indulged in by both, 'till my brain
Fairly reeled with excitement, I grew so enchanted
With the Charming Young Widow I met in the Train.

4. *We became so familiar I ventured to ask her*
How old was the child that she held at her breast.
"Ah Sir!" she responded, and into tears bursting,
Her infant still closer convulsively pressed,
"When I think of my child I am well nigh distracted
Its Father—my Husband—oh my heart breaks with pain."
She choking with sobs leaned her head on my waistcoat—
Did the Charming Young Widow I met in the Train.

5. *By this time the Train had arrived at a Station*
Within a few miles of the great one in town
When my charmer exclaimed, as she looked through
*   the window,*
"Good gracious alive! why there goes Mr. Brown.
He's my late Husband's Brother—dear Sir would you kindly
My best beloved child for a moment sustain?"
Of course I complied—then off on the platform
Tripped the Charming Young Widow I met in the Train.

6. *Three minutes elapsed when the whistle it sounded*
The Train began moving—no Widow appeared.
I bawled out "Stop! Stop!" but they paid no attention
With a snort, and a jerk, starting off as I feared.
In this horrid dilemma I sought for the hour—
But my watch! ha! where was it? where, where was my chain?
My purse too, my ticket, gold pencil-case—all gone!
Oh that Artful Young Widow I met in the Train.

7. *While I was my loss thus so deeply bewailing*
The Train again stopped and I "Tickets please" heard.
So I told the Conductor while dandling the infant
The loss I'd sustained—but he doubted my word.
He called more officials—a lot gathered round me—
Uncovered the child—oh how shall I explain!
For behold 'twas no baby—'twas only a dummy!
Oh that Crafty Young Widow I met in the Train.

8. *Satisfied I'd been robbed they allowed my departure*
Though, of course I'd to settle my fare the next day.
And I now wish to counsel young men from the country
Lest they should get served in a similar way
Beware of Young Widows you meet on the Railway
Who lean on your shoulder—whose tears fall like rain.
Look out for your pockets in case they resemble
The Charming Young Widow I met in the Train.

1. I live in Ver-mont And one morn-ing last sum-mer, A let-ter in-form'd me my
2. Yet scarce was I seat-ed with-in the com-part-ment, Be-fore a fresh pas-sen-ger

Un-cle was dead, And al-so re-quest-ed I'd come down to Bos-ton As he'd
en-ter'd the door, 'Twas a fe-male a young one and dress'd in deep mourn-ing An

left me a large sum of mo-ney it said; Of course I de-ter-min'd on mak-ing the
in-fant in long clothes she grace-ful-ly bore, A white cap sur-round-ed a face oh so

jour-ney And to book my-self by the "first class" I was fain Tho' had I gone
love-ly: I nev-er shall look on one like it a-gain I fell deep in

"second" I had nev-er en-count-er'd The Charm-ing Young Wi-dow I met in the Train.
love o-ver head in a mo-ment, With the Charm-ing Young Wi-dow I met in the Train.

Popular heroes,

a tearful victim,

an enviable bon vivant

On, and on, and on he goes,
Never a doubt or danger knows,
King of the Road, he's nothing to fear,
Ho, for the Faithful Engineer.

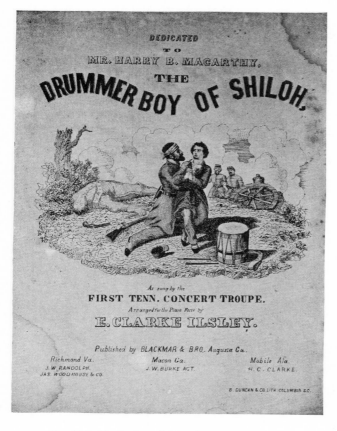

On Shiloh's dark and bloody ground,
The dead and wounded lay,
Amongst them was a drummer boy,
That beat the drum that day.

A wounded soldier raised him up,
His drum was by his side,
He clasped his hands and raised his eyes
And prayed before he died.

Oh the fireman's heart is bold and free,
His motto is to save,
He works without reward or fee,
Hurrah! for the fireman brave.

CHAMPAGNE CHARLIE.

COMIC SONG

FOR CHAMPAGNE CHARLIE IS MY NAME, CHAMPAGNE CHARLIE IS MY NAME
GOOD FOR ANY GAME AT NIGHT, MY BOYS, GOOD FOR ANY GAME AT NIGHT.

CHAMPAGNE CHARLIE IS MY NAME, CHAMPAGNE CHARLIE IS MY NAME
GOOD FOR ANY GAME AT NIGHT, MY BOYS, WHO'LL COME AND JOIN ME IN A SPREE.

Some survive, but most songs die

Although presented to the public in delightful gift wrappings, now collectors' items, the songs themselves generally faded rapidly into obscurity. A few caught on to live as part of the folk music of America. One famous survivor, "The Flying Trapeze" (1868), became a favorite with circus clowns and later enjoyed a revival by such popular singers as Walter O'Keefe and Rudy Vallee. It is still familiar to singing Americans everywhere and, with the possible exception of "The Drummer Boy of Shiloh," a favorite of Civil War buffs, is the only song from this selection to have passed the test of the years. Musical Americana publications have published a facsimile of this classic in their series of *One Hundred Great American Songs*. The version at left is one of three which appeared during the song's first year—a not uncommon publishing occurrence in those days before copyright. The parody is apparent in the substitution of a girl for the man on the trapeze. The last chorus goes:

She floats through the air with the greatest of ease,
You'd think her a man on the flying trapeze,
She does all the work while he takes his ease,
And that's what's become of my love.

In pre-Freudian days, when an ankle was an aphrodisiac, "Matilda Toots or You Should Have Seen Her Boots" enjoyed its brief moment. The heroine was having her boots laced on when she fell in; she married her rescuer—still in the same boots. Time has mercifully forgotten Matilda.

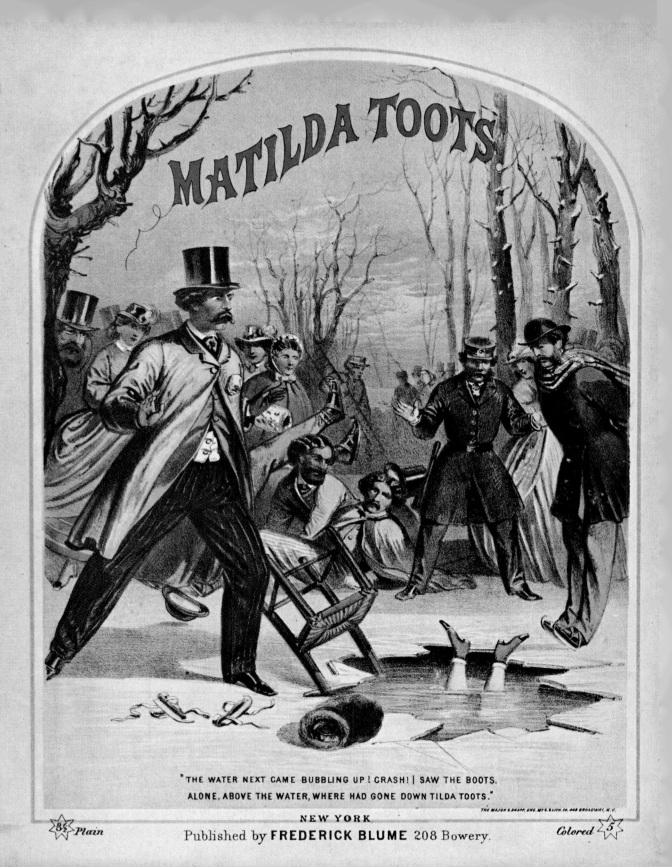

MATILDA TOOTS.

"THE WATER NEXT CAME BUBBLING UP! CRASH! I SAW THE BOOTS,
ALONE, ABOVE THE WATER, WHERE HAD GONE DOWN TILDA TOOTS."

NEW YORK,
Published by FREDERICK BLUME 208 Bowery.

THE MAJOR & KNAPP, ENG. MF'G & LITH. CO. 448 BROADWAY, N.Y.

8½ Plain

Colored 5

This is the relined Jefferson portrait acquired in 1937, which Orland Campbell believes was painted by Gilbert Stuart in 1805.

The case of the Missing

Thomas Jefferson paid Gilbert Stuart

21 years for delivery. A fire-blackened

later raises doubt that the original

"Nobody, my darling, could call me a fussy man;
But I do like a little bit of butter to my bread."

Like A. A. Milne's wistful king, Thomas Jefferson could be pardoned for feeling entitled to just a little consideration. The sage of Monticello, sometime inventor, author of the Declaration of Independence, former President of the United States, and purchaser of 828,000 square miles of Louisiana Territory, was experiencing the same kind of frustration that comes to king and commoner alike.

In 1800 Gilbert Stuart had painted Mr. Jefferson's portrait. In 1805 he had done another. Mr. Stuart had been paid for his first effort; but as of August 9, 1814, Thomas Jefferson had received neither portrait.

The former President reached for pen and paper and addressed a letter to the artist in Boston.

"You wished to retain the portrait which you were so kind as to make of me," he wrote, ". . . until you should have time to have a print copied from it. This I believe has been done, at least I think I have seen one which appeared to have been taken from that portrait. Mr. Delaplaine of Philadelphia is now engaged in a work relating to the general history of America, and, wishing it to be accompanied with prints, has

asked permission to have one taken from the same original, adapted to the size of his volume. I have therefore authorized him to ask for the portrait in your possession, to copy his print from it, and return it to me."

If Mr. Jefferson thought this rather oblique approach would succeed, he was mistaken. Four years later he was trying another tack, this time through his friend and former secretary of war, Henry Dearborn, in Boston. Somewhat testily, Jefferson asked Dearborn: "Can you without involving yourself in offense with Stewart [*sic*] obtain thro' any channel a frank and explicit declaration on what ground he detains my portrait? in what term? And whether there is to be an end of it. I think he has now had it 10 or 12 years. I wrote him **once** respecting it, but he never noticed my letter."

Less than **three** weeks later, Dearborn replied. "As there has been a much greater intimacy between my Son and Stewart [*sic*] than between Stewart & myself," he wrote, "I requested my son to call on him and endeavor to obtain such frank & explicit information from him as you desire. An interview took place and after many trifling excuses for the long detention of

Portrait

$100 for a portrait, then waited

canvas discovered over a century

ever left the artist's Boston studio

By RICHARD M. KETCHUM

This is Campbell's re-creation of the portrait found by X ray under the surface portrait opposite and believed painted by Stuart in 1800.

the portrait and its unfinished situation, he said that he could not finish it in cold weather but would certainly complete it in the Spring. We will endeavor to push him on. . . ."

Undoubtedly this came as something of a shock to a man who had waited, thus far, eighteen and thirteen years respectively for the delivery of either of two portraits, but there is no record of Jefferson's reaction.

Spring came and went, and on June 24, 1819, Dearborn wrote once more to the gentleman at Monticello. "Having not yet been able to prevail on Stuart to finish your portrait I suspect that you have paid him in part or in full in advance if so I should like to know it, as I might in that case address his pride with some chance of success. If you have not made any advance and will authorize me to pay him as soon as he shall

At left is the Campbell acquisition, before relining. The center sketch shows how the 1805 portrait (in blue) was painted over that of 1800 (in black). The 1801 English engraving (right) was copied from Stuart's 1800 portrait.

63

complete it I will address his poverty which is now great and by engaging to pay him and by frequent calls I should hope to succeed."

This was too much. Jefferson must have replied almost as soon as he received Dearborn's message, for on July 5, 1819, he sent off this firm note: "With respect to Mr. Stuart, it was in May, 1800 I got him to draw my picture, and immediately after the last sitting I paid . . . him his price, one hundred dollars. He was yet to put the last hand on it, so it was left with him. When he came to Washington in 1805 he told me he was not satisfied with it, and therefore begged me to sit again, and he drew another which he was to deliver me instead of the first, but begged permission to keep it until he could get an engraving from it."

Again the months passed until on January 20, 1820, the disgusted Dearborn took pen in hand once more. "After frequent promises," he reported to Jefferson, "Stuart has again forfeited his engagement to finish your Portrait. . . . Feeling a little out of patience I observed to him that I would inform you that you must never expect to have it." To this the slippery Stuart had replied that Jefferson had "paid him an hundred dollars for one that you [Jefferson] now have in your home . . . but that he received nothing for the one he now has. That he painted this for himself. That he had no commission from any one to paint it. I was too much out of temper to say anything more to him and retired."

If Dearborn was disgusted, Jefferson was just plain mad. On February 5 he replied in the plainest possible language: "On the subject of Mr. Stewart and my portrait, he must have spoken without reflexion, when he supposed it in my possession and hanging in my hall. The peculiarities of his temper and ideas render him a difficult subject to handle. . . . With respect to the 1st canvas portrait [the 1800 painting] I thought it a good one, and should have been content with it, had he not himself been dissatisfied with it, and still if he chuses to deliver that instead of the 2nd [the 1805 painting] if he will finish and deliver it I shall be satisfied."

Possibly mistrusting his own temper, Dearborn sent his son around to Stuart's studio a second time to see what the artist had to say. Apparently Jefferson's remarks hit home, for the painter "now owns that he had been mistaken and that he has received one hundred dollars for the portrait, which you have not received and only wants to know whether you would prefer a common portrait or one of half the length of the Body, the former at $100, the latter $300."

To this astonishing request, the former President replied with remarkable equanimity. Apologizing to Dearborn for the protracted negotiations he had had to undergo, Jefferson believed the end might be in sight at last. "We may now hope to close it," he wrote, "by accepting one of the alternatives [Stuart] proposes. I shall be perfectly content to receive the original he drew in Philadelphia in 1800, which was of the common size (that the painters call I believe a bust). It will suit me better than a half length as it will range better in the line of my other portraits not one of which is halflength." Then, remembering the artist's capacity for allowing mundane details to escape him, he added, "I have no doubt Mr. Stuart's justice will think me entitled to the original and not merely a copy. There was something pleasanter in the aspect of that portrait than the second drawn at Washington. It will come safest by water addressed to the care of Capt. Bernard Peyton, Richmond."

Finally Dearborn received a letter of acknowledgment from Monticello, dated August 17, 1821: "The portrait by Stuart was received in due time and good order, and claims, for this difficult acquisition, the thanks of the family." So far as Dearborn was concerned, the matter was closed for good. But was this, after all, the end of the story?

History has a way of not touching most of us personally, even though we smile at an exchange of letters like this and delight in the knowledge that great men are also subject to tribulations. But to Orland Campbell, a New York portrait artist, the foregoing correspondence had considerable significance.

In 1937 Campbell had come into possession of a neglected portrait of Thomas Jefferson. His first thought was that it was the work of Gilbert Stuart, and after having it relined, cleaned, and repaired, he was convinced of it. But how to prove it? His brother Courtney became interested in the picture and began searching out the scattered documents which, with evidence provided by the painting itself, eventually led the Campbells to a far more important conclusion.

As an experienced portraitist himself, Campbell also believed that the picture had been painted from life, or, in other words, that it was not a copy of Stuart's work. Examining the surface of the painting, Campbell detected several layers of paint and decided to have it X-rayed and photographed under infrared light. These tests showed immediately that there was, beneath the visible portrait, *another* likeness of Thomas Jefferson.

Jefferson's letters indicated plainly that he had not received the 1800 painting, for which he had paid Stuart one hundred dollars. In 1805, when Stuart received a commission from James Bowdoin to paint a portrait of Jefferson, the artist found himself in a terrible dilemma. He could hardly ask the President to

CONTINUED ON PAGE 85

64

"Every one of us was seized by his future master..."

A Journal
of an Indian Captivity
during Pontiac's Rebellion
in the year 1763,
by Mr John Rutherfurd,
Afterward Captain, 42nd Highland Regiment

Perhaps the most haunting fear of the American frontiersman was capture by the Indians, an experience of suffering which left a permanent mark on those who were lucky enough to survive it. As long as the Indian threat persisted, captivity accounts appeared constantly. One of the most remarkable examples of this uniquely American literary genre was written by a seventeen-year-old Scot named John Rutherfurd, who was captured near Fort Detroit during the Pontiac Rebellion of 1763. Published obscurely in the nineteenth century, his exciting account is today all but forgotten. It comes to AMERICAN HERITAGE from a New York book dealer, Miss Emily Driscoll, and has been edited by a noted authority on the history of the Great Lakes region, Dr. Milo M. Quaife, of Highland Park, Michigan.

AMERICAN HERITAGE BOOK SELECTION

ILLUSTRATED BY RAY HOULIHAN

The best-organized and most formidable Indian uprising of the eighteenth century was the rebellion of the tribes of the Great Lakes and Ohio Valley in 1763, led by the Ottawa chief, Pontiac. Less than three years after the surrender of the last French army in North America, France's former Indian allies struck the frontier in a well-planned and co-ordinated series of attacks. In all, ten British forts were captured in little more than a month, and for over a year settlements were ravaged from New York to Virginia. So serious was this outbreak that for a time the region beyond the Appalachian Mountains was closed to settlement by royal edict.

If the ferocity of the Indians seems appalling today—what John Rutherfurd witnessed was not exceptional—it must be remembered that Pontiac's Rebellion was, in a real sense, a primitive religious crusade. Already resentful of tactless handling by their English masters, and afraid of the encroachment of white settlers on their hunting grounds, the Indians were only too willing to listen to self-styled mystics who preached union of all tribesmen west of the Appalachians and a return to the older pastoral way of life.

Perhaps the most notable event of this rebellion was Pontiac's unsuccessful siege of Fort Detroit, which John Rutherfurd witnessed as a prisoner in the Indian camp. An orphan, the young Scot had come to Detroit to live with a trader named James Sterling, who was a business partner of his uncle. Early in May, 1763, he joined a survey party on a trip to Lake Huron. Unfortunately, what began as a sporting sojourn in the Michigan wilderness was to end in a protracted nightmare.

Major Gladwin of the 80th Regiment, commanding officer of Detroit, being desirous to know whether the lakes and rivers between that place and Michilimackinac were navigable for vessels of a greater burden than the small bateaux they then made use of—by which discovery Michilimackinac and the little posts thereupon depending might be more conveniently and expeditiously supplied with provisions and military stores—ordered Lieutenant Charles Robertson of the 77th Regiment, who commanded the King's vessels on Lake Erie, to go with a party consisting of six soldiers and two sailors in a large bateau with the necessary implements to sound the Lakes.* Sir Robert Davers, who had passed that winter at Detroit (excepting some little excursions he made among the Indian villages in the neighborhood), having a curiosity to see farther into the country—which in fact was the motive that induced him to come so far as Detroit—accompanied Captain Robertson; and both gentlemen inviting me to go along, I joyfully accepted their invitation as it had then all the appearance of a pleasure jaunt. We promised ourselves excellent sport in shooting water fowl, with which that country abounds, not in the smallest degree dreading any interruption from the savages around us, who but a little before in full council had renewed their profession of friendship for the English and received from them presents to a considerable amount.

* Robertson's mission was to determine whether the St. Clair route to Lake Huron was navigable for sailing ships. Although the British had the beginnings of a naval force on Lake Erie, no ships were as yet maintained on the upper Lakes.

We accordingly set out on May 2, 1763. Captain Robertson, myself, and the military party were in the bateau; Sir Robert Davers with a *panee*, or Indian slave, was in a little wooden canoe, being better than a bateau for going into shallow water after game, and so easily navigated that he and his boy were sufficient to cross the lakes and go up the creeks, among the Indian villages.*

May 4th. We overtook a canoe with an Indian family in it. We exchanged our bread and tobacco with them for fish newly caught and parted very good friends.

May 5th. We passed several Indian villages, but there appeared to be few Indians at them. We supposed they were out upon their hunting parties, but afterwards found that they were on a party of a very different nature, being collected at the place where we were afterwards attacked by them.

May 6th. In the morning we arrived at La Pinnierre where there were some Canadians building a sawmill for whom we brought, at the desire of a French gentleman at Detroit, a few barrels of flour.† They returned us thanks, and told us with all the rhetoric they were masters of that all the nations of Indians around were in league to take up the hatchet against the English; that they knew of our coming that way, and were waiting six miles up the river to seize and destroy us; and

---

* One of the first and most unfortunate "dudes" on the western frontier, Sir Robert Davers of Suffolk, England, was touring the Great Lakes "on a voyage of curiosity."

† La Pinnierre (the Pinery), on the Pine River, was the principal source of building timber for French Detroit.

if we proceeded any farther we would certainly be cut to pieces. They begged us with tears in their eyes for God's sake to return, and by means of the wind and strong current of the river, we might gain the fort before they could perceive we had discovered their intentions.

This was friendly advice given by people who showed, even by their countenances, that they had our safety very much at heart; and had we followed their counsel, many would have saved their lives on this occasion and others would have avoided a long and dangerous captivity. Captain Robertson partly doubted

". . . the Indians seeing Captain Robertson killed and the confusion we were in, rushed on us and easily boarded us."

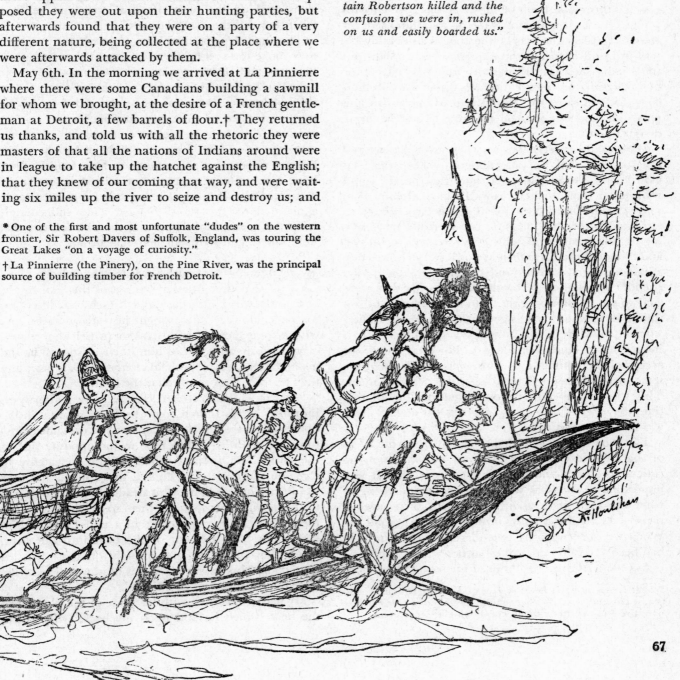

the truth of what the Canadians told us, and partly imagined they would not dare to attack us till under cover of the night. As it was then morning, he thought that he might go six miles farther and sound about the mouth of the River Huron *—which done, his work would be finished—and then return to the fort as fast as possible. He therefore ordered the rowers to ply their oars, and without seeming to suspect any danger proceeded till we came within six miles of the above river, where there was a small Indian village at the same place where the Canadians had informed us we would be attacked by the savages.

Then it was, though alas too late, that Captain Robertson discovered the truth of the information we had got; for the whole bank of the river was covered with Indians to the amount of three or four hundred. Sir Robert Davers, who was at the time considerably before us in his canoe, at the request of the Indians put the head of his canoe on shore and smoked a pipe of friendship (as they called it) with some of their chiefs till we came up. He advised us to row on and pass him, and not to seem to suspect their having a design upon us.

Here I must observe that the river was narrower and ran so rapid that we were obliged to keep the boat close to the shore; and even there the Indians could walk faster than we could row. To have attempted to return would have been inevitable destruction to us all; besides, they had all their canoes ready for pursuing us. This we were sensible of, so we kept rowing on and humored them as much as possible. They crowded about us, men, women, and children, giving us the friendly appellation of brothers, telling us they were glad to see us, and begging us to come ashore and we should have whatever was good, the squaws, or Indian women, showing us fish, maple sugar, &c, in order to induce us to land. We did not, however, choose to accept of their invitation or presents. They asked for some of our bread and tobacco, which we gave them. This was only to take up our attention, for all this time they were filing off by degrees, till at last there was not an Indian to be seen.

The squaws were collected so closely upon the bank of the river, endeavoring to divert our attention by ridiculous stories and immodest gestures, that it was impossible to see what was going on behind them or what the men were about, who were then posting themselves behind a rising ground a little beyond us. When we came opposite that place, the squaws, as it had been preconcerted, ran off as fast as they could.

As soon as they were all out of the way, the warriors

* That is, the St. Clair River at present-day Port Huron, Michigan. It must be noted that here and in several other places in the narrative Rutherfurd's estimates of distance are inaccurate.

fired upon us at the distance of about sixty yards. Captain Robertson was immediately wounded in the left side, which, showing me, he called to the men to sheer off; but alas! he had just spoken the words when another shot through his body killed him. I then took the helm and endeavored to bring the boat around, but two of the soldiers being now killed, the remaining five could not navigate the boat; and as they neither had their arms ready nor loaded, they thought only of screening themselves the best way they could from the enemy's fire; but this was all in vain, for the Indians seeing Captain Robertson killed and the confusion we were in, rushed upon us and easily boarded us, at the same time, according to their custom upon such occasions, making the most dreadful cries and yellings, what they call the *death hollow*.

They had changed their dress from what it was when they spoke to us as brothers, having at that time their blankets and ornaments on, whereas now they were naked and painted black and red, making a very frightful appearance. Every one of us was seized by his future master; for by their custom whoever first seizes a captive by his hair, to him he belongs, and none may take him from him. I was laid hold of by one whose hideous appearance was enough to have banished any hope of obtaining quarter; but indeed before this I had given up all hope of being saved and became, in a manner, resigned to the worst. They immediately scalped Captain Robertson and the two soldiers that were killed, and stripped them naked.

My master—for as such I was to acknowledge him— at that time dragged me out of the boat by the hair of the head, into the water, which took me up to the neck. However, he brought me safe on shore, and with a rope adorned with trinkets (which they always carry with them to war to bind their prisoners) bound me and delivered me over in charge of his squaw; and then he went back to plunder the boat.

All this while, Sir Robert Davers (as I was afterwards informed by his Indian boy, who was with him in the canoe) upon seeing the Indians attack us, endeavored to escape with his light canoe to the opposite side of the river. The Indians called to him repeatedly to come on shore and give himself up to them, and they would not hurt a hair of his head. He paid no regard to them, which exasperated them so much that two of them leveled their pieces at him and brought him down. His body fell out of the boat into the river, which they picked up and brought on shore, cut his head off and buried his body. His head was also buried after the scalp was taken off.

My master returned with his share of the plunder of the boat, which he laid upon my back; with which,

68

marching through the village, we came to the hut where he lived. We had not been there long, when a great many Indians came in and got drunk upon some shrub they had got as part of the plunder; and, as I knew that in their cups they often killed one another, I thought myself in as much danger as ever. One of them, dressed in Captain Robertson's clothes, came in very drunk, and seeing me lying in a corner with my hands tied, gave a *hollow,* calling out *English dog,* and made a stroke at me with his tomahawk which must have killed me, had not an Indian more sober (and whom I afterwards found to be the best of them) seized his arm and prevented him, and then turned him out of the hut.

My master's wife, seeing the danger I was in, and knowing the same or more Indians might return to the hut, made me lie down behind her, and covered me with skins and furs. Soon afterward the same Indian returned and demanded me from my master, saying *no English dog should be left alive,* upon which he was turned out a second time and well kicked. Soon after

"... *a great many Indians came [into the hut] and got drunk upon some shrub they had got as part of the plunder....*"

that a party of them came for me, upon which my master was obliged, in order to save me, to tell them I had been carried to another hut, which satisfied them.

The whole night they kept drinking what little liquor we had brought with us and making a most hideous yelling, dancing, and singing while they were feasting upon Captain Robertson's body. This shocking piece of barbarity is practiced only by some of the Indian nations to the northward. The Six Nations, who use their prisoners, while alive, much worse than they do, never eat human flesh, which *they* do, not for want of food but as a religious ceremony, or rather

from a superstitious idea that it makes them prosperous in war. They teach their children to be fond of it.

The next day my master's son brought some small pieces of the body to the hut and roasted it upon a stick at the fire, and endeavored to prevail with me to eat of it, often assuring me that *Englishmen's flesh was very good to eat.* My master requested me to taste it, telling me I was never to think of going back to the English, and so ought to conform to the custom of the Indians. I told him I would obey him in everything he desired me—and even in that if he insisted—but that it was very disagreeable to me, and that that was the only command I would make the least hesitation to obey him in, and begged he would not insist upon it. Thus, by a seeming readiness to obey him, I avoided eating the body of my friend; and I believe by showing a desire to please him rather gained upon his affections.

My hands were still kept bound behind my back. This being the second day of my captivity * and not having seen any of the poor soldiers, I concluded they had shared the same unhappy fate as their captain, which added to my uneasiness, fearing that I would not be more favorably dealt with. However, to my great joy and comfort, towards the evening of that day I saw Sir Robert's Indian boy, who told me he knew of some of the soldiers being alive.

This boy, having lived long with the English and speaking the language, made me think he would desire to get free from the Indians, who used him much worse than the English did. I therefore thought I might confide in him, so I laid myself open to him and told him of a scheme I had formed of our escaping together: which was that we should both get out of our respective huts in the night time when all were asleep, meet at a certain place agreed upon and there untie each other. As he understood traveling in the woods, he would pilot us to Detroit, which was not above eighty English miles from where we then were; each of us should bring as much fish as would subsist us upon our journey thither.

He agreed to the proposal and went off with an intention, as I supposed, of meeting at the place appointed. However, towards the end of the evening I was surprised to see my master coming into the hut, looking very angry at me, and having a thin wooden

* On this day, May 7, Pontiac and sixty warriors appeared before the gates of Fort Detroit, begging admission. But the commanding officer, Major Gladwin, had been warned that the Indians concealed shortened rifles underneath their blankets, and he ordered his men to stand armed and ready for action. The Indians were allowed within the walls; but observing the unexpected show of British strength, they did nothing. Realizing that he could not take the fort by subterfuge, Pontiac proclaimed outright war two days later. In full view of the garrison, the Indians rushed upon the cabin of an English settler and scalped the inhabitants, signaling the start of a siege which would continue for five months.

post and an axe in his hand. Without saying a word, he put one end of the post in the ground and, tying the other to the roof of the hut, cut a notch in it about two feet from the ground and told me in an angry tone something I did not understand, with signs to me to lie down upon my back. Then, taking my leg a little above the ankle, he put it into the notch, against which he tied another piece of stick so close that I could not move myself to turn upon my side, and lay upon my back with my hands tied and the end of the rope drawn underneath my master's body, who lay with his squaw near me, upon a bear-skin. Thus I passed the night like a criminal just before his execution, only with the difference that I had nothing to reproach myself with, having committed no offense against my God or the laws of my country. This treatment gave me good cause to suspect the treachery of the Indian boy, who, I afterwards found, had, in order to get his freedom, disclosed my intentions.

Next morning my master loosed my leg, and by an Indian who spoke English told me he had discovered my intention of escaping; and that had I gone off, or even attempted it, death would certainly have been the consequence, showing the situation of Fort Detroit surrounded by four Indian nations, viz: Chippewas (the nation I was with), Ottawas, Potawatomies, and Wyandottes, who so blockaded the fort that nobody could come in or go out; adding that in a few days there would not be an Englishman in it alive. Whereupon I found it was absolutely necessary for my safety to affect a relish for their savage manners, and to put on an air of perfect contentment, which I had often heard was the way to gain the affections of the Indians; whereas a gloomy, discontented air irritates them and always excites worse treatment, and sometimes occasions the death of the captive who is so unfortunate as not to be able to accommodate himself to his situation. I therefore assured him I should no more think of leaving him, which so pleased him that he took me out to walk and showed me where Sir Robert was buried and what remained of Captain Robertson's body after the feast. He likewise pointed out to me how impossible it was for us to have escaped in our boat. He then took me to where the bodies of the poor soldiers lay who fell in the attack and were become food for the dogs, which were eating them.

Here he loosed my hands, and with the string bound up a heavy burden of sticks which he put on my back to carry home, telling me I was always to do that, or whatever work his wife desired me. When I was delivered of my burden, he again tied my hands and fastened the rope to the rafters of the hut, but did not put my leg in the stocks as on the night before. It was

equally impossible for me to escape, but by this time I had given up all hopes of effecting it, unless a more favorable opportunity should offer.

Next morning my master and his family went off in his canoe to join the rest of the warriors encamped at Detroit, leaving me to the care of his father, who seemed fond of me and wished that I should become a savage as soon as possible. Soon after my master's departure, his father stripped me of my clothes and told me I should wear them no more, but dress like an Indian. He accordingly gave me a blanket and breechclout, which is a piece of blue cloth about a yard and a half long and a foot broad which they pass through betwixt their legs, bringing each end under a belt which is round the middle for that purpose. Then he shaved my head, leaving only a small tuft of hair upon the crown and two small locks, which he plaited with silver brooches interwoven, making them hang over my face which was painted with a variety of colors. He likewise made me a present of a tobacco pouch and pipe, telling me I should smoke. I did, and afterwards became fond of it.

The hunting season being at this time past, the Indians lived upon fish, without either bread, butter, or salt. This did not agree with my constitution, so that having suffered much from a dysentery, I became so weak as to be unable to walk for seven or eight days, during which time the old man consoled me by telling me that I should not be eaten if I died of that disorder. Ten days after this my master returned with his family; and after much talk of the success of their arms against the English, how many prisoners they had taken, &c, he looked at me, turning me round about, and seemed surprised to see me dressed *en sauvage*. He asked for my hair, which the old man giving him, he put carefully by. Still my hands were tied, and whenever I had occasion to go out an Indian boy held the end of the rope, and when he brought me in, fastened it to the rafters of the hut again.

My master soon after this untied my hands, often telling me of the impossibility of my escaping. I told him I had no such intention, and feigned a satisfaction with their way of living and a particular fondness for my new dress, by which means I secured his good will, as he thought he was sure of me, and that from my being so young I would sooner take to the novelty of their way of life and more easily forget my country and my friends. Certain it is, by this behavior I fared in many respects better than those prisoners who appeared sullen and displeased with their situation, some of them suffering death on that account.

I now frequently saw two of the soldiers that were taken with me, but the Indians did not choose us to have long conferences together. However, these short meetings now and then were very satisfactory. It gives inexpressible pleasure to meet one of your countrymen when in a foreign country; judge how much more so when in captivity with a nation of savages of a different color from ourselves. Happy was I to meet and converse with these poor fellows, who a little before I would not suffer to speak to me without the usual marks of respect from an inferior to a superior. Here there was no distinction; nay, we were glad to find three people of our color. We used often to compare notes with regard to the usage we met from our masters. One of them told me he was obliged to eat of Captain Robertson's body. We would form fifty different ways of making our escape, and immediately reject them all as impracticable.

About the middle of May we were in great distress for want of provisions, owing to the indolence of the savages, who never stir out of their huts to fish or hunt till necessity drives them, which was our case at this time. During four days the wind continued so high that no fish could be taken, as they durst not venture upon the lake with their little bark canoes, which generally are navigated by two men (or a man and a boy), the former standing in the bow, or fore part, where there is a pole fixed having a light at the end, which attracts the fish; it being in the darkest nights they are most successful. The man in the bow sees the fish approaching and directs the boy how to steer the canoe, so that he may strike the fish with a harpoon or three-pronged gig.

In this manner I have seen as much as two men could carry of catfish, perch, and pike taken in two hours' time. Independent of the satisfaction of procuring what is so necessary a part of sustenance among them, it is a great amusement and truly a pleasant sight to see upwards of fifty of these lights moving upon the smooth lake in every direction, while the only sound heard is the different cries of wild beasts in the forest. This occasions no apprehension to the fishers, who are out of their reach. I before have observed that the stormy weather had reduced us to our last extremity, viz., picking up acorns and boiling them in ashes and water, changing the ashes and water frequently to remove the bitter taste. This was our food till the fifth day, when the wind abating, we got plenty of fish.

The Indians are so accustomed to being reduced to this shift that they think nothing of it, and are always sure to make up their loss. When they have victuals of any sort in their huts, they do nothing but eat, smoke

"... it is a great amusement and truly a pleasant sight to see upwards of fifty of these lights moving upon the smooth lake in every direction. ..."

their pipe, and sleep. Sometimes they amuse themselves with a game something like our children's diversion of shinty, where the females play against the men and often come off victorious.* It is on this occasion that the beaux and belles make their conquests and dress in their best attire. My master used to dress me out in the richest manner, putting all the ornaments belonging to the family upon me, taking me out to the plain and making me strut about to show myself when the whole village was assembled, calling out to the people to look at the little white man. At this time I was only made a show of, and not suffered to join in the game.

Towards the end of May we began to make preparations for our voyage to join the rest of the warriors encamped within a few miles of Detroit. For this purpose my master thought it necessary to build a canoe (which he and I did in two days) sufficient to carry all our family for many thousand miles. The evening before our departure I was surprised to see my master seize one of the dogs—of which animals we had several in the hut poking their noses every now and then in our victuals, which they could easily reach as the floor was the only table we had. This dog (which I was not sorry for) was killed and given over to the squaw, who scraped him, as we do a hog, in hot water. Then my master invited all his neighbors, sending a man round the village with a number of little painted sticks, one of which was left with each. Upon entering the hut where the feast is held, every one produces his bit of stick and lays it upon a platter provided for the purpose. Each of the guests got a double portion, eating one and carrying the other home in a dish which they bring with them for this purpose. I sat in the corner of the hut, a silent spectator of this feast, being looked upon as a slave and unworthy to partake of so fine a repast.

After killing, or rather drowning, another dog for

* This was the game of lacrosse, immensely popular among the tribes of the Great Lakes.

the purpose of appeasing the evil spirit (as they gave me to understand), we set out next morning in our canoe, making short daily voyages, always landing before sunset and putting up our cabin and cooking our fish, which office fell to my share, as well as cutting wood for the fire. The cabin or hut is soon made. It consists of about twenty young trees set up in the shape of a sugar loaf, and all covered with a kind of matting (which is carried in the canoe), excepting a hole in the top to let out the smoke. Every one carries his or her bed clothes on his back, which is either the skin of a wild beast or a coarse blanket; and all lie down promiscuously, men, women, and children, with their feet to the fire, which is in the center.

The second day of our voyage we came to an island where there was an Indian burying ground. Here we halted, and around a particular grave, which my master afterwards told me was that of one of his sons, he made us all plant a few grains of corn; which done, we re-embarked and went on our journey, which we ended in four days, arriving at a Frenchman's house in the neighborhood of Detroit.

This man being a friend of my master, we took up our residence close by his house rather than join the rest of the warriors, who were encamped five miles nearer the fort. We immediately set about building a large bark house more convenient than those they carry about with them. Here the fireplace was out of doors, where I broiled two hours every day, boiling their kettle with a little fish or Indian corn in it. This new house we finished in about four days, the severest part of which work fell to my share, such as carrying the wood and bark.

Here I must observe that I suffered inexpressible pain from my not having any clothes on, not so much as a shirt to protect me from the scorching rays of the sun which burned my shoulders and back so much that I was one continued blister, and the palms of my hands were in the same state from continual working with the axe. The next piece of fatigue I was put to was assisting my mistress in planting a large field of Indian corn, or maize, pumpkins, and other vegetables. This being finished, my master carried me to the grand encampment about five miles from Detroit. Here I had the pleasure of seeing Captain Campbell and Lieutenant McDougall of the 60th Regiment, who came out of the fort at the commencement of the blockade, with Major Gladwin's proposals of peace with the

Indians. To these they would not listen; on the contrary, they detained those two gentlemen prisoners at a Frenchman's house.

Upon my observing to Captain Campbell that I thought we might attempt our escape, being within sight of the fort, he told me by no means to think of it, as he was well assured that if any one escaped, the Indians were determined to sacrifice those that remained. I frequently made visits to these gentlemen, who belonged to the Ottawa nation. Every day there were prisoners and scalps brought in to the camp. The scalp is not, as is commonly believed, the whole skin of the head, but is only the uppermost part of the crown, and must have in it that swirl in the hair which every one has there before it can be approved of as a just trophy of the warrior's achievement.

They at this time brought in Ensign Pauli of the 60th Regiment, who commanded at a small fort on Lake Erie. The Indians came into his fort as friends, and while some of them were smoking a pipe as a token of pretended friendship the rest were butchering his small garrison, of whom they did not leave one alive. This gentleman made a very good Indian, being of a dark complexion, and was much liked by his master, who soon adopted him into his family, which exempted him from all drudgery.

So great a concourse of Indians gathered together in the French settlement reduced the inhabitants to great distress for want of provisions. The Indians killed their cattle, sheep, and poultry; and when these failed we were almost starved, frequently having nothing for a whole day but a single handful of Indian corn, which we parched in the ashes and ate with a spoonful of bear's grease. I often used to beg for a morsel of bread among the Frenchmen's houses, from whose doors I was frequently turned with an empty stomach. I was not able to bear this as well as the Indians, who, when thus pinched, have a way of girding their bodies with a belt, which they continue to straiten as their fast continues to be prolonged.

In this distressed situation my master prudently resolved to quit the camp, and moved us back to the

place where I was taken prisoner. Here we had fish as before, and sometimes a little venison. On our return to this village we halted near the burying ground I have mentioned, and while my mistress and I were erecting our hut, my master went out and killed a bear, which we ate of most heartily. After finishing our repast I was ordered to put the kettle again on the fire, which surprised me a little as we commonly went to sleep after eating. I ventured to ask the meaning of it, and was given to understand by looks and gestures that in the morning I should have the mystery revealed. My master then cut some of the choicest bits of the bear and put them into the kettle, which was hung over a slow fire, and we went to rest.

At day-break the next morning we were called up, and in a formal solemn manner walked up to the grave, near which a little fire was made. Having seated ourselves around it, each with our dish in our hand, my master arose and made a long speech, during which he often pointed to the grave and to me alternately. At every pause we joined in a sort of chorus by way of approving of what he said. When he had finished his speech he divided the broth and meat among us, and after saying a few words over the grave put a piece of the fat of the bear into the fire and directed us to do the same.

This, I was told, was to appease the spirit of the deceased, who might be offended at my being adopted in his place. He then told me I was as much their son as if I had sucked these breasts (showing me those of his wife), telling me at the same time to look upon the boys as my brothers, and that my name should be no more Saganash, or Englishman, but Addick, which signified a white elk. Notwithstanding this, I was generally called by my master's name, which was Peewash. I had three brothers, Mayance, Quido, and Quidabin.

My master, or rather *my father* now, frequently took me out hunting with him, which was an amusement I was very fond of. Although this was not the season for killing deer, he was under the necessity of taking a few to subsist his family upon when at the camp with the rest of the warriors. We accordingly set out for the camp when we had cured a few carcasses of venison, which we did by smoking them, having no salt.

In crossing Lake St. Clair it happened to blow pretty hard, so that our little frigate was in danger of going to the bottom with Peewash and all his family. To appease the evil spirit, he cut some handfuls of tobacco small, and threw it into the lake, at the same time making a long speech. Whether owing to the tobacco or not I shall not pretend to determine, but we got safe upon terra firma; and as the rain had wet our shirts and blankets we hung them on trees and ran about naked till they were dried. They likewise make use of that plant (tobacco) in thunder storms, throwing a quantity of it into the fire; and while it is burning a squaw drums with a piece of iron on the bottom of a kettle. This, they pretend, prevents any mischief from being done to the family by the lightning.

By this time our corn was grown up about a foot high, so that it became necessary to have it hoed and weeded, which was a severe task upon my mother and me for six days. I flattered myself that my being adopted into the family would have exempted me from this kind of drudgery, as was the case with most of the other prisoners; but Peewash, having a particular regard for his wife, chose that I should still assist her on many occasions, and she, being fond of ease, laid the most of it on my shoulders. She frequently made me pound or bruise corn in a large mortar till there was scarcely any skin upon my hands. When I showed them to her she only laughed and told me I should soon be better used to it, and that my hands would become hard like hers, which indeed were neither soft nor fine.

The men think it beneath them to do anything but fish or hunt for the support of their family, and in this they take no more trouble than is absolutely necessary. They frequently kill the game and leave it till they can send their squaws to carry it home, directing them how to find it by breaking off branches and marking the trees for miles from where the game was killed. Having found it, she brings home the choicest pieces and dresses them for her Lord and Master, who generally sleeps till he is called to get up and eat. When he has finished his repast he regales himself with a pipe of tobacco mixed with the leaves of the sumac shrub.

". . . Peewash, having a particular regard for his wife, chose that I should assist her on many occasions, and she, being fond of ease, laid the most of it on my shoulders."

73

In the meantime the rest of the family are busy roasting fish or broiling steaks, each one for himself. The steaks are broiled or toasted upon the end of a stick as we toast bread, and in my opinion this is the most delicious way of eating roast meat. Sometimes our mother roasted a large piece for the whole family. As the outside becomes a little done, everyone with his knife falls upon it and slices away as it roasts, by which means the pleasure of eating (which is one of their chief gratifications) is prolonged. When soup is made, or rather when they boil their fish or meat, they hang the kettle up out of the reach of the dogs, for every one in their turn to drink as they choose. The want of salt made me for some time think whatever I ate was very insipid and tasteless. However, hunger and custom prevailed over prejudice and I soon came to eat as heartily as Peewash himself.

About the 8th of June Lieutenant McDougall with a Dutch trader made their escape into the fort,* which caused them to look more strictly after us that were left with them, particularly Captain Campbell, who was shut up in a garret in a Frenchman's house. I frequently visited him with Peewash. One evening he told me he felt unwell, and was prepossessed with a notion that he was to die very soon. I endeavored to persuade him not to encourage a thought so melancholy and dispiriting, but to my great grief and sorrow the first thing I heard next day was that he had been killed.

* Actually, McDougall escaped the night of July 1; Captain Campbell was murdered but three days later.

That morning Captain Hopkins of the Rangers made a sortie from the fort, attacked a party of Indians, and killed one of the chiefs of the nation to which I belonged. The friends of the deceased were resolved to be revenged by killing an English captive. This they could not do more conveniently than by murdering poor Campbell, who belonged to the Ottawa nation. That nation, in their turn, was enraged against the Chippewas for killing their prisoner, whom they were fond of, and resolved upon having satisfaction, which could only be obtained by sacrificing a prisoner belonging to the Chippewas of rank equal to that of Captain Campbell, the better to compensate the loss. Accordingly they pitched upon Ensign Pauli, but he being informed of his danger by a handsome squaw who was in love with him, assisted by her escaped out of the Frenchman's house; from whence with much difficulty he got into the fort after being fired at several times by the sentries, who took him for an Indian.

The Ottawas, disappointed in their design upon Pauli, determined to take my life—being, as they thought, next in rank to an officer and superior to any of the private soldiers they had among them. Peewash, hearing that they were in search of me, took me to a Frenchman's barn and covered me with straw, in which situation I lay for the space of three hours, expecting every moment to have the tomahawk in my skull, till a party of Indians, with Peewash at their head, came and took me out of the barn. Notwithstanding his assuring me I was not to suffer death, I could not help being doubtful of my safety.

"Here in the road was lying a dead body, mangled and scalped, which the dogs were eating."

They marched me as a prisoner for four miles till we reached the grand encampment, which was in the middle of the French settlement. Here in the road was lying a dead body, mangled and scalped, which the dogs were eating. They made me stop for a considerable time, and looked at it with much seeming satisfaction, at the same time in an exulting tone of voice telling me that there lay our chief, our *Great Chief,* Captain Campbell. Indeed it would not have been possible for me to have recognized that it was the remains of my good friend. He was scalped and his ears, nose, an arm, a leg, and other parts of his body cut off. It was a very shocking spectacle to me; yet however disagreeable, I was obliged to view it.

They then led me into a great hall in a Frenchman's house, in the court yard of which there were about two hundred Indians of different nations. In the middle of the hall a small table and five chairs were placed, in four of which sat the chiefs of the nations encamped around Detroit; the fifth chair was for myself, who at that time would gladly have dispensed with this mark of distinction.

They then produced some letters written in English; and Pontiac, the leading man of the four nations, told me by a French interpreter that as I could speak French and read English writing they had pitched upon me to explain what was in these letters; which he ordered me to do without concealing any part of them, threatening me with death if I did not read them verbatim as they were written. Then one of the prisoners, a native of Virginia who had been fond of an indolent life and married among them, told me that he could read English and would overlook the papers and discover if I attempted to conceal any part of them, adding that the consequence would be my being scalped on the spot.

I accordingly set to work and read the letters in French to a Frenchman, who explained them to the Indians. They were only some old letters that Captain Campbell had in his pocket when he was killed, and a few letters to him from his friends at Detroit, sent from thence by a Frenchman who, instead of delivering them, had kept them.

There were several French gentlemen in the hall, who were all as eager about reading the letters as the Indians. What both French and Indians wanted to know was whether peace was declared with France or not. It had been publicly declared by Major Gladwin in Detroit long before that time, but the Canadians could not bring themselves to believe that *Le Grand Monarch* [Louis XV] would ever cede their country to Great Britain. They still flattered themselves that if they could excite the savages to maintain the war against us for a little while, a reinforcement might come to their assistance from France, and that the English might be driven out of Canada; and they were in hopes that there might be something in the letters that might favor their design.

Accordingly they always told the Indians that Major Gladwin had only declared peace in order to prevent their making war upon the English. The letters, however, contained nothing that I thought could favor their design; notwithstanding, they found means to construe them differently, and at least made the Indians more doubtful of the truth of what had been told them by Major Gladwin. When I had done they all thanked me and appeared satisfied with my proceedings and gave me leave to return home with Peewash, who told me he was glad he brought me off so well.

The next memorable circumstance that happened to me was my being sold to Monsieur Cuillerier, with whom I had been well acquainted before my captivity, and during it had been frequently at his house (which was only two miles from Detroit) with Peewash in order to get a little bread and salt. In these visits I proposed to Monsieur Cuillerier to endeavor to purchase me from Peewash, who I knew was covetous and fond of riches in the Indian way of estimating wealth, which consists of possessing a profusion of trinkets, such as wampum, beads, bracelets, and silver gorgets.

This gentleman, on account of Mr. Sterling, with whom he was very intimate (and who afterwards married his daughter), was much my friend. He made several offers to Peewash for me, by bringing with him a horse and a cow, thinking they would do, as he had often said that he liked the white people's manner of living and enjoying such comforts; but he had a greater liking for me than to part with me at so small a price. However, he agreed to let me go for certain merchandise, such as he should choose, to the value of £40, upon condition that I was always to live with Monsieur Cuillerier and not to be allowed to go back to the English.

This we both promised, although we only intended to keep it so long as it would be attended with no risk to my benefactor to break it, for rather than that he should suffer, I was resolved to live with him, although at the risk of being again seized by the savages. My mother and brothers took a very affectionate leave of me, and went home loaded with the goods they had got for me, leaving me overjoyed with my change of situation. I immediately threw away my dirty, greasy, painted shirt, which I had worn for two months without ever being washed. I scrubbed myself for two hours with soap and warm water to get the grease and paint off. Then dressing myself *en Canadian* with a clean French shirt and long ruffles, a new breech clout, with a mantlet exactly like our lady's bedgown, and a pair of new leggings, I began to feel somewhat comfortable.

This Frenchman being a brother to the former French commandant, and a very great favorite of the Indians, they had favored him a little by not killing all his stock, such as cattle, poultry, &c. So I got a good supper genteelly served up, went to a good bed which was provided for me, and slept better than I had done for a long while before. I awoke next morning happy in the thought of being out of the hands of the savages and once more, as I imagined, restored to liberty, thinking there was no doubt I would soon be among my friends in the fort. At the worst, to live with such a good family till the war ended would be but a slight hardship. But how fleeting are the joys of this life, and how uncertain are we weak mortals of what it may please the Almighty that we shall suffer in this state of trial and probation. I was happy at this moment beyond expression, and in the next I was doomed to misery.

Before sunset, as I was enjoying the company of the amiable Mademoiselle Cuillerier, lamenting together the miserable situation of many poor captives that were still in the hands of the Indians and contriving methods for the deliverance of some of them, a party of armed Indians entered the house—all of them Ottawas and consequently strangers to me—and without saying a word to me or any of the family seized me in a rude manner and brought me down stairs. Then, indeed, my situation wore a very gloomy appearance. I was hurried away from that good family without having time to say more than farewell to them who, on their part, were as much amazed as myself.

They dared not interpose in my behalf, nor attempt to save me. The ladies of the family burst into tears, crossed themselves several times, and, I believe, fervently prayed for me. All that Monsieur Cuillerier could say to me was to desire me to keep up my heart, and trust *en le Bon Dieu.* As we passed by the French houses, all the inhabitants were pitying me, saying what a sad thing it was to behold so young a lad come to so untimely an end; others were calling to me to keep up my spirits, saying there were still hopes, &c, &c. As for myself, I own I was at first much shocked when they seized me; but by degrees I became more resigned, and began to think seriously that my time was at last come, and the dangerous escapes I had made were as so many warnings to me to prepare for that change which we must all undergo sometime or other.

They carried me to Pontiac's hut—the chief of the Ottawas—who, after leaving me in suspense for some hours, procured a French interpreter who informed me the reason he took me from Monsieur Cuillerier was because several Dutch traders had got Frenchmen to buy them, or rather ransom them, as I had done, and if he suffered that trade to go on they would soon have no captives; therefore he was resolved either to keep us all, or else our scalps, for which reason he had ordered all that had been so bought to be taken from them that had purchased them, and that he had resolved to keep me for himself.

This speech eased me in some measure of the disagreeable apprehensions I was under, and gave me reason to hope that my last hour was not so near as a little before I had imagined; yet I wished again to be in Peewash's family. However, this night I remained with Pontiac, but early the next morning the Chippewas, the nation I formerly belonged to, sent a party to take me from the Ottawas; but Pontiac, having somehow taken a liking to me (I believe owing to my youth, for they seldom grow fond of elderly people who have the misfortune to fall into their hands, from a belief that they never will be reconciled to their manner of life), refused to deliver me up, the consequence of which refusal had nearly been a war between the two nations.

This was prevented by Wasson, the chief of the Chippewas. After a good deal of altercation upon the subject, Pontiac thought it most prudent to deliver me up, and thereby avoid a war with a nation superior in number to his own, which, besides the possibility of destroying his own nation, would have infallibly ruined the common cause for which they were united. I was immediately carried off by King Wasson to his hut. He was very good to me. He gave me plenty of victuals, and he told me he had plenty of girls in his family to do all the work, so that I should never be asked to do anything, but live as he and his sons did.

This pleased me very much, and indeed the behavior of him and his family was such that I had reason to think myself fortunate in falling into his hands. Every member of the family, which was very large, vied with one another to show me the most countenance and favor, and when any disturbance or alarm appeared in the camp, such as the young fellows, out of mere wantonness or in a drunken frolic, killing any of the captives—which they too frequently did—I was always hid till the danger was over.

The old king became so fond of me that he offered to make me his son-in-law when I should be disposed for matrimony and should fancy any of his daughters, who were reckoned the handsomest in the camp, and had more wampum than any others. He was satisfied with my telling him that I thought myself highly honored by the proposed alliance; and although I was not inclined to take a wife at that time, I did not know how soon I might wish to change my condition, and that then I should be happy to choose one of his family.

Little did I suspect that the ease and tranquility I then enjoyed would be of so short duration. I had not been in this situation for ten days when Peewash expressed a desire to have his son back again with him, saying that he and his wife had heartily repented their selling me to the French gentleman. They were willing to return the merchandise they had received for me, providing I was again restored to them, adding that it grieved their hearts to see me in the possession of another.

Wasson, however great his desire to keep me in his family, knew that although he was the chief of the nation he had no power to keep what was another's property. He likewise did not choose to expose himself or his family to the revenge of Peewash, who would take the first opporunity to resent the injury done him. He therefore was obliged to give me up to my father, who with his whole house received me again with joy and the most expressive marks of satisfaction, while that of Wasson seemed sorry to part with me, and even the princesses showed that they were not indifferent.

The number of prisoners increased every day. Towards the end of July they had upwards of fifty, besides a great number of scalps that were daily brought into the camp; they were every day murdering some of their prisoners, even those that had been as long among them as myself. One day, in particular, I was in the hall of a Frenchman's house, which was crowded with Indians, when some of the young warriors brought eight naked captives into the hall, at the sight of which I was surprised and terrified. I asked an Indian who was of the same nation with myself, and who had frequently professed a regard for me, whether or not I was to fall a sacrifice with those they were about to murder. At this question, he was amazed to see me there; and without making any answer he hurried me through the crowd, and putting me into another room in the house charged me to lie close and make no noise, otherwise I would be discovered and killed. He then locked the door and left me to think on what had passed.

I found two Dutch merchants in the room in the same situation as myself, having been hid there by their masters, who were desirous of saving them from the fury of their brethren. During our confinement we heard the Indians making long speeches over the unhappy people that were to suffer, telling them it was in order to make them prosperous in the war against the English that they were to be killed. The poor victims were begging the French people, who were looking on, to intercede in their behalf. One little boy in particular, a drummer of the Rangers about twelve years old, was crying bitterly and imploring their mercy; but alas, he knew not how vain it was to ask it from wretches whose hearts were steeled against every feeling of humanity.

I ventured to crawl to the window, where I saw them lead to the riverside (which ran just by the house) eight of these poor creatures, one by one, whom they put to death on the spot. Some of them were tomahawked, others they shot with their guns, and some of them they made the little boys shoot with bows and arrows, in order to accustom them to cruelty and perfect them in the use of that weapon. Thus they prolonged the pain of these unhappy wretches, and when one fell, the multitude would set up the most dreadful yells and cries that can be conceived. When they were all dead they scalped them, and some of the Indians took the skin off their arms to make tobacco pouches of (as they had formerly done with Captain Robertson and Captain Campbell), leaving the first joints of the fingers by way of tassels.

Then they threw the bodies into the river that they might float down to the fort, where their countrymen might see what they said they should all undergo in a short time. When this tragical scene was at an end, the Indian that had hid me came and set me at liberty, first leading me publicly through the middle of the crowd to convince me that there was no more danger at that time. Then he delivered me to Peewash, who seemed very happy to see me safe, having heard that the warriors had been hunting to destroy me.

The following reason was given for this last instance of their barbarity. An old squaw, the wife of a chief, dreamed that she saw ten English men killed and scalped. This she told to the young warriors, who wished for nothing more than a pretext to make a frolic of that sort. She conjured them at the same time to make her dream come true, otherwise, she assured them, they would never prosper in war. This, with a great deal more enthusiastic stuff mixed in her speech, excited their passions to such a degree that they flew immediately about the camp like mad men to collect ten of the prisoners in order to kill them, in the manner I have related, to verify the dream of that imp of hell.

However, they were partly disappointed in their design, as all those who had any regard for their captives concealed them. The little drummer was the favorite of an old squaw, who wanted much to save him, but notwithstanding her tears and earnest entreaties the young fellows tore him from her arms, declaring that upon such an occasion they would spare neither age nor sex. Almost every day exhibited fresh instances of their barbarity upon some of the prisoners, so that I lived in continual terror, expecting that every day would be the last. I therefore resolved to attempt escaping at all risks.

There lived a Frenchman near where we had our cabin named Boileau. This man had been civil to me upon several occasions, and I thought he might be of some assistance to me in making my escape. I therefore sounded him upon the subject and found that a little money would go a great way with him. Accordingly I promised to reward him if he would assist me, and thereby gained him to my service. As the French were admitted into the fort, I gave him a letter to my friend, Mr. Sterling, who likewise promised him a reward if he should succeed in delivering me from my captivity. Major Gladwin and several other officers also assured him of their countenance.

When he returned with a line from Mr. Sterling, I found him ready to engage in my interest. I therefore redoubled my entreaties and promises in case of success. A scheme for my departure in the most secret manner was next to be fixed upon. We formed many, but rejected them all upon more coolly considering the matter. Our eagerness—he to enjoy the promised reward and I, what was more important, my liberty—made it difficult for us to determine upon the most practicable way of effecting it.

However, we at last determined upon the following plan: in the evening we should fix upon, he was to embark in his canoe, giving out publicly that he was going fishing as usual; instead of which, he was to go about two miles down the river nearer the fort, and at a certain point of low land which was covered with rushes, he was to push into the place in the dusk of the evening when the Indians would not perceive him, and so conceal himself. I, on my part, was to make the best of my way to him in the night, where he would lie waiting for me.

This plan we were to put into execution the following night. However, on this and several preceding nights the Indians were alarmed by a report that the Chippewas were to be attacked by our forces, which actually happened a few days afterward. Captain Dalzell, who had just brought a reinforcement to the garrison of Detroit, in the night of July 30–31 made a sortie with a strong body of men, with the intention of surprising the hostile camp. But the Indians, who had been warned of his design by the French, lay in ambush and attacked him with great spirit; nay, upon this occasion they did what savages were never known to do, they threw themselves into the houses and annoyed the British troops very much from there and from behind fences. The battle continued doubtful for some time; but at last our troops were obliged to retreat, which they did in good order to the fort, leaving upon the field Captain Dalzell and about sixty private soldiers.

Peewash knew nothing of the intended attack till the firing of the artillery and small arms roused him from his sleep. As soon as he heard it, he got up in a great hurry and put on his powder horn and pouch. He then tied my hands, lest in the confusion I should make an attempt to kill the women in the family and make my escape, after which he took his gun and ran as hard as he could to join the army with his party, which was about two miles from where we lived. About two hours afterward he returned to us, overjoyed with the success of the day, giving a most pompous description of the battle and making out that vast numbers of British soldiers were killed, while only six of the Indians had fallen. He likewise told me that our *sugema,* or great chief, was slain, meaning Captain Dalzell.

I was now unbound and sent to another hut for a large wooden mortar to pound corn in. The Indian to whom I went for it had likewise been in the engagement, and was boasting of his feats prodigiously. He told me he had taken the heart of our great warrior, which he would soon feast upon, showing me poor Dalzell's heart roasting at the fire, pieces of the fat of which the young men took off, and in my presence rubbed it on the mouth of a poor soldier of the 60th Regiment whom they had taken prisoner. This, and other barbarities committed upon prisoners taken in the action, shocked me so much that I went directly to Monsieur Boileau's under pretence of bringing some bread to our hut, and agreed to meet him the next night at the place appointed, after having repeated and enlarged my promises of reward to him.

When the evening came I lay down as usual upon my bear skin to sleep, putting off all my ornaments: wampum, silver bracelets, collar, etc. About the middle of the night when I guessed that the family were all fast asleep, I crawled out of the hut on all fours. When I was outside, I stood at the door for five minutes to hear if they were stirring, but as everything was still I thought this was my time to set off, which I did as fast as my feet could carry me, directly to the woods. I had no other clothes than my shirt, not even daring to put on a pair of moccasins to save my feet, for if the family had happened to awake, they would immediately have come after me; and if they had found me dressed, they would not be long in discovering my intention.

In all my life I never saw such a night of rain, thunder, and lightning. It was so dark, and the woods were so thick and full of briars and thorns, that I was very much retarded in my progress. I could scarcely make more than a mile in an hour. I therefore resolved upon a new method, and quitting the woods I went to the river which was hard by, in which I thought I could walk with the water up to my chin, so that the Indians on the road could not see me. This plan would have succeeded had I had more time, but I had yet four miles to go before I could reach the Frenchman, and was in danger of being surprised by daylight.

I therefore resolved to take to the woods again, but I was within an ace of being prevented, for just as I was going ashore I saw two Indians with their guns, in close conference. They passed by on the road within twenty yards of me. Fortunately there was an old tree which had fallen into the river close by me, behind which I immediately squatted; but I could not conceal myself altogether, so that they must have seen me had they looked that way. If they had observed me, I never would have gotten out of that spot alive. I knew this and was in dreadful apprehension, as several soldiers attempting to escape were caught, scalped, and tomahawked on the spot. But these Indians, fortunately for me, were engaged in earnest discourse, and were returning from a feast a little intoxicated. I saw them go into a little French house about one hundred yards from me. I immediately ran to the thicket, making as little noise as possible; and to prevent the whiteness of my skin from discovering me to the Indians I rubbed myself all over with black moss and mire.

Thus pursuing my journey in fear and hope, starting at every rustling among the leaves and often mistaking trees for Indians, I at last arrived at the place where I thought the Frenchman would be waiting with the canoe, but could not find him. I ventured to call out in a low voice, but nobody answered. I then began to exclaim against the perfidy of the Frenchman, who, in my desperate situation, I thought had deceived me. Being much exhausted with fatigue, I sat down to rest, hardly knowing what I did. My thoughts were occupied about the Frenchman who, upon reflection, I thought would not be such a coward as to abandon me when he knew that I had to go through the most dangerous part of the enterprise myself. I considered, likewise, that it was to his interest to carry out our agreement. Recollecting myself a little and looking around me, I discovered what my anxiety had made me overlook, that I was about a quarter of a mile higher up the river than the place we had appointed.

This discovery gave me fresh vigor and spirit. I soon

". . . I thought this was my time to set off, which I did as fast as my feet could carry me, directly to the woods. . . ."

reached the right place, and to my inexpressible joy, I found the man asleep in his canoe. After waking him we embarked and pushed to the middle of the river in order that the current might carry us down. We passed through the middle of the enemy's camp, making as little noise with our paddles as possible. We could plainly hear them talk, and saw some of them dancing and singing at a feast around a fire. About an hour before day-break we arrived on board a ship lying opposite to Detroit.

Then it was that I was agitated in a manner I had never before experienced. It would be in vain to attempt to give an idea of my feelings on this occasion. In the morning I went to the fort, where my friends were overjoyed to see me, although I cut a very odd figure among civilized people. The whole town, inhabitants as well as the garrison, turned out to see me. My appearance was sufficient to excite their pity as well as their laughter. I had on nothing but an old greasy, painted shirt, my face was painted red, black, and green, my hair had been cut off, and my body was black with the moss I had put on. My thighs and legs were so torn by the briars and thorns and so affected by the poisoned vines that they were swollen as big as any grenadier's in His Majesty's service.

Monsieur Boileau went home as soon as he had put me on board the ship, fearing that if he did otherwise he would be suspected of having aided me in my escape, and this was the last sight I had of him. Mr. Sterling, by my order, gave him goods to the value of £23 which, with the £39 10s. given by Monsieur Cuillerier when he bought me (of which scarcely any was returned when I was retaken), amounted to £62 10s. Pennsylvania currency, which is equal to £39 sterling.

After I had been about ten days in the fort and had got the better of my fatigues (though not of the paint), one of the vessels sailed for Niagara to obtain a supply of provisions for the garrison. Mr. Sterling had obtained leave of Major Gladwin to have a considerable quantity of goods that were lying at Niagara brought to Detroit in the vessel, and having no proper person whom he could trust to oversee their safety, he applied to me. I knew that bringing up these goods would be of considerable advantage to the company, and wishing to do what little was in my power for the advantage of a company with which my uncle was connected, I agreed to run the hazard, and accordingly embarked on board the sloop.

We had some shots fired at us by the Huron Indians going down the river, which we returned. In four days we arrived at Fort Schlosser, near the Falls, and marched under a strong guard to Niagara without any interruption from the enemy. It was late before the sloop was loaded and ready to sail again. Some artillery stores and provisions, with about 18 officers and soldiers of the 17th and 46th Regiments, was the chief loading.

We had only sailed one day when the vessel sprung a leak and was half full of water before it was discovered. All of the pumps were of little use, so that after throwing all the heavy artillery and some other things overboard, we found the only way to save our lives was to crowd sail for the land and run the vessel on shore; but every one seemed to think she would go to the bottom before we could reach land.

Dread and consternation was painted on every countenance, and I was surprised to find myself the least moved of all, which must have been owing to my having been for some time so much exposed and inured to danger. While some were stripping themselves to swim, others cursing and swearing at their companions for not working, others praying, and some drinking brandy, I looked tamely on, after finding I could be of no assistance.

When we were at the worst and everyone thought we were going down, our boat, which was our last resource, broke adrift. Our prospect was now truly dismal, expecting every minute to sink or be dashed to pieces on the rocks. I may truly say that the cries and shrieks of a naval officer's lady with three children affected me much more than my own condition. It was a pitiful sight indeed. The mother held two of her children in her arms while the other little innocent was making a fruitless attempt with her hands to stop the water from rushing into the cabin, already some three inches deep. She did this, she said, to prevent the water from drowning her mama.

At last, to the inexpressible joy of all on board, the vessel struck upon a bank of sand within fifty yards of the shore. The difficulty now was how to get ashore, where we had much reason to wish ourselves, as we feared the high surf of the lake would dash us to pieces. In this situation we would have been much at a loss had not Captain Montresor of the Engineers bravely undertaken to swim ashore. Although the distance was great with a high sea and the danger of Indians being there, he accomplished it and brought the boat back, by which means we all got safe to land.

Expecting the Indians would attack us, we fortified ourselves the best way we could with the barrels of provision. The necessity for this soon appeared, for we were soon attacked by a large body of them, who had watched our motions for some time, waiting till we should be more off our guard, which we in fact were at that time.

Several of us were walking along the shore of the lake when we were alarmed by the cries of the savages,

"I agreed to run the hazard, and accordingly embarked on board the sloop."

which made us take to our heels and endeavor to gain the breastwork as fast as possible. I very nearly fell into the hands of the enemy again upon this occasion, as I had happened to stray from the rest of my companions. They rushed out of the woods upon one poor soldier of the 60th Regiment, who happened to be nearer them. He knocked down the first savage who reached him, but the second cut him with his tomahawk, which felled him to the ground. Neither that nor their scalping deprived him immediately of life. As soon as the Indians left him for dead, he got up and staggered toward the foot of the hill. The Indians were still firing upon us, and not a man dared venture to bring the poor fellow up the hill, who by this time had become insensible. We frequently called to him, but he paid no attention and wandered a little farther, where some days later, when the Indians were gone, we found him dead under an old tree.

For my own part, I had much ado to regain the top of the hill. I was hotly pursued, and in my flight, in scrambling through the bushes, both my shoes fell into their hands. This was a loss I regretted but little. As soon as we reached the breastwork they fired very hot upon us, which we returned. Our works being very open, we had several of our men killed. The Indians left us the next day, but we were detained upon this spot, which we called Lovers Leap, for twenty-four days before we could get a reinforcement of bateaux to carry us back to Niagara. It was here I first entered upon duty as a military man. Every one took his turn of duty as a common soldier. We marched over the carrying place at the Falls of Niagara just three days after the Indians had defeated our troops, and saw there about eighty dead bodies, unburied, scalped, and sadly mangled.*

* These were the victims of the massacre at Devil's Hole, a spectacular chasm in the Niagara River Gorge. At this time a wagon road ran along one edge; and here a British supply train was ambushed by Indians on September 14, 1763. Those white men who were not struck down on the spot were forced over the precipice, along with horses and wagons; only three escaped. Hearing the sound of distant rifle fire, a party of soldiers rushed to help, and was in turn ambushed and nearly wiped out.

When at Niagara, I resolved to tempt fortune no longer in the woods, and determined to go to New York. I arrived here a few days ago, where I expect to remain for some little time with my uncle, and afterwards join the 42nd Regiment, in which I have just got an ensigncy, preparing for an expedition against the Shawnee and Delaware Indians to the westward under the command of Colonel Bouquet. . . .

I wish you may be able to understand this long, illwritten narrative, which I have written in a great hurry, as when I began I had no idea that I should have swelled it out to the size of a pamphlet. However, if I had had more time, I don't think that I should have put it into much better language, for having so long been confounded with hearing and speaking different languages, French, Dutch, Chippewa, Ottawa, &c &c that it is no wonder I should be at a loss to write or speak that of my native country.

Ill-prepared for a siege of any duration, Pontiac's Indians were unable to take Fort Detroit; by the end of September, 1763, they were eager to sue for peace. Winter was coming, morale was ebbing, ammunition running out, and expected aid from the French posts in Illinois had been refused. On October 12 Gladwin granted a truce and Pontiac withdrew from the Detroit area. Meanwhile, in Pennsylvania, Colonel Henry Bouquet had routed a large Indian force at Bushy Run and relieved a beleaguered Fort Pitt. Although Indian depredations on the frontier continued for another year, these reverses all but broke the spirit of the conspiracy.

As for John Rutherfurd, little is known of his later life. On his return to New York he enlisted in the famous 42nd Highland Regiment, known as the Black Watch, and was probably a member of Bouquet's Ohio River expedition of 1764, which obtained peace treaties from the Indians of that region. Rutherfurd fought with the Black Watch during the Revolution, rose to the rank of captain, and after thirty years as a career officer retired to a small property, Mossburnford, in Roxburghshire, Scotland. He died there in 1830, aged 84.

READING, WRITING, AND HISTORY

By BRUCE CATTON

A Man Withdrawn

We like to make thumbnail sketches of our famous men, and to Henry David Thoreau we have given one of the most compact of the lot. We see him as the complete lone wolf, the man who tried to reform the world by divorcing himself from it and reforming himself. Declaring that a free man could not without disgrace associate himself with a government that would make war on Mexico in the interest of the slavocracy, he went to jail rather than pay taxes; then he built a hut by Walden Pond and lived there in complete isolation, creating his own world when the world other men had created seemed unsatisfactory.

This sketch has the merit of brevity, and it is drawn from life; after all, Thoreau himself provided the outlines. But it is incomplete, for Thoreau kept changing, and he refused to stop thinking after his sabbatical in the lonely cabin; and Leo Stoller tries to bring him into better focus in his perceptive essay, *After Walden*.

Thoreau's divorce from the world, Mr. Stoller points out, was only temporary. He lived for fifteen years after the Walden experiment, and he developed new ideas. Secession from human society, obviously, came to seem an inadequate answer, and the government which he had disowned finally won his ardent support when at last it got to the point of making war on disunion and slavery. Furthermore, his ideas on economic man underwent considerable expansion.

To become a subsistence farmer (generations before the term was invented) was simple enough, in the

1840's. Beyond Walden Pond there was an open continent, and it was easy to argue that a man could leave society if he chose and strike out for himself. Nevertheless, industrial capitalism and the infinitely complex institutions that go with it were then coming into being, and it was finally necessary to accept it rather than to run away from it. The Walden experiment might help a man get his personal life in order, but it was not a permanent answer. Thoreau returned to the world, supporting himself as the rest of us must do —that is, he got a job: which, in itself, raised problems. He objected bitterly to the way New England was

---

After Walden: *Thoreau's Changing Views on Economic Man,* by Leo Stoller. The Stanford University Press. 163 pp. $4.

---

destroying its forests, his beloved wilderness areas; yet his own work as a surveyor was contributing to the process.

His goal remained the same: man should strive for the simple life, "the object of life is something else than acquiring property," and salvation continues to lie within. But he seems to have become less certain about the means by which the goal could be reached. He came to see (as Mr. Stoller puts it) that "the preindustrial economy itself was no guarantee of a true simplicity," but to find a place for simplicity amidst a growing industrialism began to look very difficult. The Walden experiment had failed; there was no economic foundation for Thoreau's doctrine.

"Thoreau could not longer advise mankind to resign

from the industrial and agricultural revolutions and head for the woods," says Mr. Stoller. "Neither, however, could he reconcile his individualism with any form of socialism. He was left with a critique of industrial and commercial civilization but with no associated program of action."

Individualism, then, was not, by itself, quite enough. In the beginning Thoreau's assumption was that men lived after all pretty much as they chose to live, and that if they did not take proper advantage of their own freedom of choice it was their own fault. But he could see that it was necessary to live in America as it was; perhaps, therefore, even the best individualist had to give some thought to ways in which the existing society could be improved. If self-culture was to be attained it would have to be won within industrial society and by means of it.

Obviously, this line of thought leads one to the point where sooner or later he must embrace organized political action, and this point Thoreau never quite managed to reach. He was coming to see that "the success of the single man in his private life was dependent on the success of the community of men in their social life," but his social thought was transitional. He never worked his way through to a final solution; and yet, as Mr. Stoller aptly remarks, "perhaps we are mistaken in asking completion and should rather be satisfied with growth."

Reformer's Role

Thoreau's growth was in the grand tradition. He shared to the full in the New England Puritan heritage, which compels men to a constant re-examination of the responsibility which the righteous man owes to society. From the earliest beginnings around Massachusetts Bay, there has always been the question: When society follows a course which you consider morally wrong, do you then withdraw from society (thus keeping your own principles intact), or do you get into the thick of things and try to shape society into a better form? John Winthrop had to grapple with the problem two centuries ahead of Thoreau, and his course is examined in Edmund S. Morgan's thoughtful book, *The Puritan Dilemma*.

Puritanism, as Mr. Morgan says, created in men and women an almost unendurable tension. It required a man to devote his life to the search for salvation, but it also taught him that he was really helpless to do anything but evil; he must reform the world, but the world's evil was incurable. As governor of Massachusetts Bay Colony in its all-important formative years, Winthrop faced the problem "of living in this world

without taking his mind off God." Withdraw from the world he could not; he had to stay on the firing line and do his best.

Not for Winthrop were Thoreau's doubts about the extent to which a man should try to modify the society about him. Every nation (as Winthrop kept insisting) existed by virtue of a covenant with God, in which it promised to obey God's commands. Government had

---

The Puritan Dilemma: *The Story of John Winthrop,* by Edmund S. Morgan, edited by Oscar Handlin, Little, Brown and Company. 224 pp. $3.50.

---

a sacred task and enjoyed divine sanction in carrying it out, but the citizen was not thereby absolved from responsibility. If government lived up to its high commitment the citizen must support it, but if it should fall from grace the citizen must be ready to go on the warpath and replace it with a better government. He must also keep an eye on his neighbor.

A colony dedicated to such principles could not be an easy one to govern, for the line that separates such dedication from pure cantankerousness can be very thin. But it did have remarkable possibilities for development, and some of these possibilities, in Massachusetts Bay, were fully exploited. If men are bound to have a government which is bound by God's laws, they must decide for themselves what sort of government that is to be and then they must create it. Winthrop saw to it that the colonists were able to do this—and, without quite realizing it, thereby carried the budding nation a long step in the direction of democracy.

He had his problems, among them one posed by Roger Williams, who in his seventeenth-century way was something like Thoreau: a man perfectly willing to withdraw from an imperfect society and go start a new one on his wild lone. When Winthrop prayerfully urged the young man to reconsider his notion that everyone but Williams was out of step, Williams retorted: "Abstract yourselfe with a holy violence from the Dung heape of this Earth." From a perfectionism of this sort Winthrop consistently abstained. But the community to which he gave so much expert guidance was bound to develop men who felt that way.

The Massachusetts Bay experiment did not come out quite as Winthrop had anticipated. In a way, it succeeded; that is, as Mr. Morgan says, it "came as close as men could come to the Kingdom of God on earth." But when it had attained this success—around 1640—it found that England, the mother country for whose guidance this difficult task was being performed, was looking the other way. The world was no longer watching . . . and thus the whole colony was on the verge of turning its collective back on the world and following a separatism of its own, stepping off into complete, self-satisfied isolationism. Against such a step Winthrop set himself. The rest of the world might indeed be lost in sin, but it had to be lived in and with; not even in a New World which they were shaping by the dictates of their own consciences could men escape from their responsibilities. To do right in a world gone wrong, man must remain in the society of his fellows.

Great Debate

Among the men who accepted this notion without hesitation were those two nineteenth-century leaders, Abraham Lincoln and Stephen A. Douglas. In 1858 they went straight to the hustings for a hand-to-hand grapple with a burning political question which, boiled down, was the question of the continued existence or the containment and ultimate extinction of chattel slavery. They debated the issue, in a series of the most famous political arguments in American history, each man doing his best to bring about the political action that would make America a better land; and the complete record of their debates is made available in *Created Equal?* edited and with an uncommonly penetrating introduction by Paul M. Angle.

Created Equal? *The Complete Lincoln-Douglas Debates of 1858,* edited and with an introduction by Paul M. Angle. The University of Chicago Press. 460 pp. $7.50.

Both Lincoln and Douglas deserve the title, "statesman," and in these debates they were doing what statesmen are supposed to do, but do not often do: that is, they were taking the hottest issue of the day and bringing it directly to the people, discussing it from the same platform so that an informed electorate might at last come to an intelligent decision. Yet something escaped them—or, perhaps, lay beyond the boundaries of the democratic process itself. For these notable debates did not finally settle the issue that engaged them. They did settle a state election, to be sure, and they had much to do with determining how a subsequent national election would go—but within three years the nation had given up debating the issue and had taken to fighting about it, getting into a four-year war whose incidental costs are still with us.

And a reader of the text can hardly fail to be struck by the fact that for all their thoroughness in debate both men stayed away from the fundamental issue that lay beneath the slavery issue itself: How, in a nation

dedicated to freedom and democracy, do black and white races finally get along with each other? If slavery ends, what relationship takes its place? Are all men created equal, no matter what the color of their skins, and if they are, how do they go about living together? With this question the debaters refused to grapple.

Resort to Force

When debate fails, action comes; and an instructive companion book to Mr. Angle's is the excellent *First Blood: The Story of Fort Sumter,* by W. A. Swanberg.

Mr. Swanberg stations himself right where the dam finally burst—at Charleston Harbor, in South Carolina—and examines the course of events from, roughly, the fall of 1860 to the April day in 1861 when the guns opened fire. When he begins, the United States is still one nation, rather lackadaisically maintaining certain badly run-down military installations in one of its seaports; before he gets very far the one nation has unaccountably become two, and the men responsible for these military installations (to say nothing of the men responsible for the two nations) are trying to do the best they can under conditions of unheard-of complexity and difficulty; and when he concludes the two nations have gone to war, and what could not be debated out will be fought out.

This makes a wholly fascinating story; a record of the strange, exciting, and sometimes incomprehensible things men did when a war that nobody really planned came over the horizon and became inevitable and at last actual. It is more than a simple account of the things done by soldiers and elected officials, although it gives the complete story of their doings.

First Blood: *The Story of Fort Sumter,* by W. A. Swanberg. Charles Scribner's Sons. 373 pp. $5.95.

In effect, all hope of a political solution had died, when Mr. Swanberg begins his story. Somewhere along the line—perhaps before Lincoln and Douglas ever began to debate with one another, perhaps while they were talking, perhaps afterward—the American political mechanism had broken down. A settlement had gone out of reach, and instead of trying to persuade one another, men of North and South were mounting guns around Charleston Harbor.

. . . A long step, this, from Thoreau's pious hope that a man could withdraw from an unsatisfactory world? Long enough, certainly; and the question of how man, the social animal, adjusts himself and his society to the demands of his ideals still is unanswered.

The Case of
the Missing Portrait

CONTINUED FROM PAGE 64

sit for a new portrait when the first one had never been delivered to him. Nor could Stuart copy the 1800 painting, because Jefferson had aged considerably in those five years, and his appearance was further altered by the fact that he wore his hair differently.

Faced with these problems, Stuart told Jefferson that he was dissatisfied with the first portrait and asked for another sitting. Thereupon he simply *corrected* the 1800 picture by painting a new likeness right over it, on the same canvas. This was borne out by the X rays, which showed that the artist had painted out part of the face and superimposed another on it. And the outline of the subsurface portrait revealed by these X rays bore a marked resemblance to two English engravings made from the 1800 portrait—the only copies known to have been made of it.

If Campbell's analysis was correct, the 1800 picture had disappeared from sight in 1805, at the moment Stuart painted a new likeness on top of it. This not only explained the fact that Jefferson never received it, but made clear why Stuart had been so reluctant when pressed to deliver it.

There was also a good explanation of why Stuart had not wanted to part with his 1805 study of Jefferson. In those days before photography it was common practice (and a sure source of income) for a portrait painter to execute a life study of a prominent man and then to make replicas of it for sale to as many other people as could be persuaded to buy one. Stuart, frequently in financial difficulty, referred to certain replicas as his "hundred-dollar bills," because he could count on that amount for each one he turned out.

Re-examining the X rays of his portrait, Campbell could see evidence that the picture had undergone several costume changes—changes which Campbell could match up with known copies by Stuart and other artists. Obviously, if this picture had been Stuart's original life study, or "master" painting, from which copies were made, it was the last thing in the world Stuart would want to part with.

Yet there was that 1821 letter of Jefferson's, stating that the portrait had been received at Monticello. If the picture in Campbell's possession was indeed *both* the 1800 and 1805 portraits, what had Stuart sent to Jefferson? With the permission of the owner, Campbell examined that painting carefully.

This was the famous Edgehill portrait, so named because it had been removed from Monticello after Jefferson's death and taken to adjoining Edgehill, the home of his daughter Martha.

Two things about the Edgehill impressed Campbell. First, it was painted on a wood panel—and Jefferson, in a letter to Dearborn, had referred specifically to a "canvas portrait." Second, the panel was so thinly painted over that the grain in the wood could be seen through it. In other words, this painting contained none of the costume changes discernible in Campbell's own picture. To Campbell, this indicated that no other paintings had been copied from the Edgehill and that it was not, therefore, Stuart's original life study.

Then there was the statement made in 1892 by Jefferson's great-granddaughter, Mrs. William B. Harrison. Asked about the portrait received at Monticello in 1821, Mrs. Harrison recalled her grandmother's doubt that this could be the original life portrait, since the paint was wet when it arrived.

Campbell was convinced that he had the original life portrait of Jefferson, a painting that Stuart had retained to the bitter end. And there was something else which seemed to fit his puzzle. When Gilbert Stuart died in 1828 his possessions passed to Jane Stuart, his daughter. About 25 years later her studio burned to the ground, and the fate of its contents became a mystery.

Turning once more to the painting which had set him off on a twenty-year search, Campbell looked at the charred area at the back of the stretcher and mused that this portrait had done as good a job of speaking for itself as one might expect from an inanimate object.

85

How the Frontier Shaped the American Character

CONTINUED FROM PAGE 9

frontier never served as a "safety valve" for laborers in the sense that Turner employed the term. Instead, the American frontiers were pushed westward largely by younger sons from adjacent farm areas who migrated in periods of prosperity. While these generalizations apply to the pre-Civil War era that was Turner's principal interest, they are even more applicable to the late nineteenth century. During that period the major population shifts were from country to city rather than vice versa; for every worker who left the factory to move to the farm, twenty persons moved from farm to factory. If a safety valve did exist at that time, it was a rural safety valve, drawing off surplus farm labor and thus lessening agrarian discontent during the Granger and Populist eras.

Admitting that the procession to the frontier was more complex than Turner realized, that good lands were seldom free, and that a safety valve never operated to drain the dispossessed and the malcontented from industrial centers, does this mean that his conclusions concerning the migration process have been completely discredited? The opposite is emphatically true. A more divergent group than Turner realized felt the frontier's impact, but that does not minimize the extent of the impact. Too, while lands in the West were almost never free, they were relatively cheaper than those in Europe or the East, and this differential did serve as an attracting force. Nor can pages of statistics disprove the fact that, at least until the Civil War, the frontier served as an indirect safety valve by attracting displaced eastern farmers who would otherwise have moved into industrial cities; thousands who left New England or New York for the Old Northwest in the 1830's and 1840's, when the "rural decay" of the Northeast was beginning, would have sought factory jobs had no western outlet existed.

The effect of their exodus is made clear by comparing the political philosophies of the United States with those of another frontier country, Australia. There, lands lying beyond the coastal mountains were closed to pioneers by the aridity of the soil and by great sheep ranchers who were first on the scene. Australia, as a result, developed an urban civilization and an industrialized population relatively sooner than did the United States; and it had labor unions, labor-dominated governments, and political philosophies that would be viewed as radical in America. Without the safety valve of its own West, feeble though it may have been, such a course might have been followed in the United States.

Frederick Jackson Turner's conclusions concerning the influence of the frontier on Americans have also been questioned, debated, and modified since he advanced his hypothesis, but they have not been seriously altered. This is true even of one of his statements that has been more vigorously disputed than any other: "American democracy was born of no theorist's dream; it was not carried in the *Susan Constant* to Virginia, nor in the *Mayflower* to Plymouth. It came out of the American forest, and it gained a new strength each time it touched a new frontier." When he penned those oft-quoted words, Turner wrote as a propagandist against the "germ theory" school of history; in a less emotional and more thoughtful moment, he ascribed America's democratic institutions not to "imitation, or simple borrowing," but to "the evolution and adaptation of organs in response to changed environment." Even this moderate theory has aroused critical venom. Democracy, according to anti-Turnerians, was well advanced in Europe and *was* transported to America on the *Susan Constant* and the *Mayflower;* within this country democratic practices have multiplied most rapidly as a result of eastern lower-class pressures and have only been imitated in the West. If, critics ask, some mystical forest influence was responsible for such practices as manhood suffrage, increased authority for legislatures at the expense of executives, equitable legislative representation, and women's political rights, why did they not evolve in frontier areas outside the United States—in Russia, Latin America, and Canada, for example—exactly as they did here?

The answer, of course, is that democratic theory and institutions were imported from England, but that the frontier environment tended to make them, in practice, even more democratic. Two conditions common in pioneer communities made this inevitable. One was the wide diffusion of land ownership; this created an independent outlook and led to a demand for political participation on the part of those who had a stake in society. The other was the common social and economic level and the absence, characteristic of all primitive communities, of any prior leadership structure. The lack of any national or external controls made self-rule a hard necessity, and the frontiersmen, with their experience in community co-operation at cabin-raisings, logrollings, corn-huskings, and road or school building, accepted simple democratic practices as natural and inevitable. These practices, originating on the grass roots level, were expanded and extended in the recurring process of government-building that marked the westward movement of civilization. Each new territory that was organized—there were 31 in all—required a frame of government; this was drafted by relatively poor recent arrivals or by a minority of upper-class leaders, all of whom were committed to democratic ideals through their frontier community experiences. The result was a constant democratization of institutions and practices as constitution-makers adopted the most liberal features of older frames of government with which they were familiar.

This was true even in frontier lands outside the United States, for wherever there were frontiers, existing practices were modified in the direction of greater equality and a wider popular participation in governmental affairs. The results were never identical, of course, for both the environment and the nature of the imported institutions varied too greatly from country to country. In Russia, for instance, even though it promised no democracy comparable to that of the United States, the eastward-moving Siberian frontier, the haven of some seven million peasants during the nineteenth and early twentieth centuries, was notable for its lack of guilds, authoritarian churches, and all-powerful nobility. An autocratic official visiting there in 1910 was alarmed by the "enormous, rudely democratic country" evolving under the influence of the small homesteads that were the normal living units; he feared that czarism and European Russia would soon be "throttled" by the egalitarian currents developing on the frontier.

That the frontier accentuated the spirit of nationalism and individualism in the United States, as Turner maintained, was also true. Every page of the country's history, from the War of 1812 through the era of Manifest Destiny to today's bitter conflicts with Russia, demonstrates that the American attitude toward the world has been far more nationalistic than that of non-frontier countries and that this attitude has been strongest in the newest regions. Similarly, the pioneering experience converted settlers into individualists, although through a somewhat different process than Turner envisaged. His emphasis on a desire for freedom as a primary force luring men westward and his belief that pioneers developed an attitude of self-sufficiency in their lone battle against nature have been questioned, and with justice. Hoped-for gain was the magnet that attracted most migrants to the cheaper lands of the West, while once there they lived in units where co-operative enterprise—for protection against the Indians, for cabin-raising, law enforcement, and the like—was more essential than in the better estab-

lished towns of the East. Yet the fact remains that the abundant resources and the greater social mobility of frontier areas did instill into frontiersmen a uniquely American form of individualism. Even though they may be sheeplike in following the decrees of social arbiters or fashion dictators, Americans today, like their pioneer ancestors, dislike governmental interference in their affairs. "Rugged individualism" did not originate on the frontier any more than democracy or nationalism did, but each concept was deepened and sharpened by frontier conditions.

His opponents have also cast doubt on Turner's assertion that American inventiveness and willingness to adopt innovations are traits inherited from pioneer ancestors who constantly devised new techniques and artifacts to cope with an unfamiliar environment. The critics insist that each mechanical improvement needed for the conquest of the frontier, from plows to barbed-

wire fencing, originated in the East; when frontiersmen faced such an incomprehensible task as conquering the Great Plains they proved so tradition-bound that their advance halted until eastern inventors provided them with the tools needed to subdue grasslands. Unassailable as this argument may be, it ignores the fact that the recurring demand for implements and methods needed in the frontier advance did put a premium on inventiveness by Americans, whether they lived in the East or West. That even today they are less bound by tradition than other peoples is due in part to their pioneer heritage.

The anti-intellectualism and materialism which are national traits can also be traced to the frontier experience. There was little in pioneer life to attract the timid, the cultivated, or the aesthetically sensitive. In the boisterous western borderlands, book learning and intellectual speculation were suspect among those dedicated to the material tasks necessary to subdue a continent. Americans today reflect their background in placing the "intellectual" well below the "practical businessman" in their scale of heroes. Yet the frontiersman, as Turner recognized, was an idealist as well as a materialist. He admired material objects not only as symbols of advancing civilization but as the substance of his hopes for a better future. Given economic success he would be able to afford the aesthetic and intellectual pursuits that he felt were his due, even though he was not quite able to appreciate them. This spirit inspired the cultural activities—literary societies, debating clubs, "thespian groups," libraries, schools, camp meetings—that thrived in the most primitive western communities. It also helped nurture in the pioneers an infinite faith in the future. The belief in progress, both material and intellectual, that is part of modern America's creed was strengthened by the frontier experience.

Frederick Jackson Turner, then, was not far wrong when he maintained that frontiersmen did develop unique traits and that these, perpetuated, form the principal distinguishing characteristics of the American people today. To a degree unknown among Europeans, Americans do display a restless energy, a versatility, a practical ingenuity, an earthy practicality. They do squander their natural resources with an abandon unknown elsewhere; they have developed a mobility both social and physical that marks them as a people apart. In few other lands is the democratic ideal worshiped so intensely, or nationalism carried to such extremes of isolationism or international arrogance. Rarely do other peoples display such indifference toward intellectualism or aesthetic values; seldom in comparable cultural areas do they cling so tenaciously to the shibboleth of rugged individualism. Nor do residents of non-frontier lands experience to the same degree the heady optimism, the rosy faith in the future, the belief in the inevitability of progress that form part of the American creed. These are pioneer traits, and they have become a part of the national heritage.

Yet if the frontier wrought such a transformation within the United States, why did it not have a similar effect on other countries with frontiers? If the pioneering experience was responsible for our democracy and nationalism and individualism, why have the peoples of Africa, Latin America, Canada, and Russia failed to develop identical characteristics? The answer is obvious: in few nations of the world has the sort of frontier that Turner described existed. For he saw the frontier not as a borderland between unsettled and settled lands, but as an accessible area in which a low

man-land ratio and abundant natural resources provided an unusual opportunity for the individual to better himself. Where autocratic governments controlled population movements, where resources were lacking, or where conditions prohibited ordinary individuals from exploiting nature's virgin riches, a frontier in the Turnerian sense could not be said to exist.

The areas of the world that have been occupied since the beginning of the age of discovery contain remarkably few frontiers of the American kind. In Africa the few Europeans were so outnumbered by relatively uncivilized native inhabitants that the need for protection transcended any impulses toward democracy or individualism. In Latin America the rugged terrain and steaming jungles restricted areas exploitable by individuals to the Brazilian plains and the Argentine pampas; these did attract frontiersmen, although in Argentina the prior occupation of most good lands by government-favored cattle growers kept small farmers out until railroads penetrated the region. In Canada the path westward was blocked by the Laurentian Shield, a tangled mass of hills and sterile, brush-choked soil covering the country north and west of the St. Lawrence Valley. When railroads finally penetrated this barrier in the late nineteenth century, they carried pioneers directly from the East to the prairie provinces of the West; the newcomers, with no prior pioneering experience, simply adapted to their new situation the eastern institutions with which they were familiar. Among the frontier nations of the world only Russia provided a physical environment comparable to that of the United States, and there the pioneers were too accustomed to rigid feudal and monarchic controls to respond as Americans did.

Further proof that the westward expansion of the United States has been a powerful formative force has been provided by the problems facing the nation in the present century. During the past fifty years the

American people have been adjusting their lives and institutions to existence in a frontierless land, for while the superintendent of the census was decidedly premature when he announced in 1890 that the country's "unsettled area has been so broken into by isolated bodies of settlement that there can hardly be said to be a frontier line" remaining, the era of cheap land was rapidly drawing to a close. In attempting to adjust the country to its new, expansionless future, statesmen have frequently called upon the frontier hypothesis to justify everything from rugged individualism to the welfare state, and from isolationism to world domination.

Political opinion has divided sharply on the necessity of altering the nation's governmental philosophy and techniques in response to the changed environment. Some statesmen and scholars have rebelled against what they call Turner's "Space Concept of History," with all that it implies concerning the lack of opportunity for the individual in an expansionless land. They insist that modern technology has created a whole host of new "frontiers"—of intensive farming, electronics, mechanics, manufacturing, nuclear fission, and the like—which offer such diverse outlets to individual talents that governmental interference in the nation's economic activities is unjustified. On the other hand, equally competent spokesmen argue that these newer "frontiers" offer little opportunity to the individual—as distinguished from the corporation or the capitalist—and hence cannot duplicate the function of the frontier of free land. The government, they insist, must provide the people with the security and opportunity that vanished when escape to the West became impossible. This school's most eloquent spokesman, Franklin D. Roosevelt, declared: "Our last frontier has long since been reached. . . . Equality of opportunity as we have known it no longer exists. . . . Our task now is not the discovery or exploitation of natural resources or necessarily producing more goods. It is the sober, less dramatic business of administering resources and plants already in hand, of seeking to re-establish foreign markets for our surplus production, of meeting the problem of under-consumption, of adjusting production to consumption, of distributing wealth and products more equitably, of adapting existing economic organizations to the service of the people. The day of enlight-

ened administration has come." To Roosevelt, and to thousands like him, the passing of the frontier created a new era in history which demanded a new philosophy of government.

Diplomats have also found in the frontier hypothesis justification for many of their moves, from imperialist expansion to the restriction of immigration. Harking back to Turner's statement that the perennial rebirth of society was necessary to keep alive the democratic spirit, expansionists have argued through the twentieth century for an extension of American power and territories. During the Spanish-American War imperialists preached such a doctrine, adding the argument that Spain's lands were needed to provide a population outlet for a people who could no longer escape to their own frontier. Idealists such as Woodrow Wilson could agree with materialists like J. P. Morgan that the extension of American authority abroad, either through territorial acquisitions or economic penetration, would be good for both business and democracy. In a later generation Franklin D. Roosevelt favored a similar expansion of the American democratic ideal as a necessary prelude to the better world that he hoped would emerge from World War II. His successor, Harry Truman, envisaged his "Truman Doctrine" as a device to extend and defend the frontiers of democracy throughout the globe. While popular belief in the superiority of America's political institutions was far older than Turner, that belief rested partly on the frontier experience of the United States.

These practical applications of the frontier hypothesis, as well as its demonstrated influence on the nation's development, suggest that its critics have been unable to destroy the theory's effectiveness as a key to understanding American history. The recurring rebirth of society in the United States over a period of three hundred years did endow the people with characteristics and institutions that distinguish them from the inhabitants of other nations. It is obviously untrue that the frontier experience alone accounts for the unique features of American civilization; that civilization can be understood only as the product of the interplay of the Old World heritage and New World conditions. But among those conditions none has bulked larger than the operation of the frontier process.

Ray Allen Billington, a member of the Advisory Board of AMERICAN HERITAGE, *is professor of history at Northwestern University. He contributes regularly to historical journals and has written several books, among them* The Protestant Crusade *and* Westward Expansion, A History of the American Frontier.

Father of our Factory System

CONTINUED FROM PAGE 39

carding machines, as well as the drawing and roving frame and the two spinning frames. At last he was ready for a trial.

Taking up a handful of raw cotton, Slater fed it into the carding machine, cranked by hand for the occasion by an elderly Negro. This engine was one of the most important elements of the Arkwright system, for in it the raw cotton was pulled across leather cards studded with small iron teeth which drew out and straightened the fibers, laid them side by side, and formed them into a long, narrow fleece called an "end," or "sliver." This was then placed on the drawing and roving frame to be further stretched, smoothed, and then twisted before being spun into yarn on the spinning frame. Before the cotton was run through the cards, the fibers lay in every direction, and it was essential that the carding be successful if the "end" was to be suitable for the subsequent steps. But when Slater fed the test cotton into his machine it only piled up on the cards.

Slater was greatly perplexed and dismayed. The machinery had already taken a long time to make, and his partners were becoming impatient. Slater sensed their growing doubts and knew he would forfeit their confidence if this first trial failed. Yet he had nobody who could check on the correctness of his designs. The Wilkinson family later described his anxiety. Standing before their fireplace, he sighed deeply, and they saw tears in his eyes. Mrs. Wilkinson, noting his distress, asked, "Art thou sick, Samuel?" Slater answered sadly, "If I am frustrated in my carding machine, they will think me an impostor."

After a number of sleepless nights, Slater determined that the trouble arose from a faulty translation of his design into reality, for Pliny Earle had never before made cards of that description. Slater decided that the teeth stood too far apart, and that under pressure of the raw cotton they fell back from their proper places instead of standing firm and combing the cotton as it moved past. He pointed out the defect to Earle, and together, using a discarded piece of grindstone, they beat the teeth into the correct shape. Another test was made and the machine worked satisfactorily.

The final stage was now at hand. Almost a year had passed in preparation for this moment. Would the machinery operate automatically by water power? That was the miracle of the Arkwright techniques, which

gave them their name, "perpetual spinning." A connection was made to the small water wheel which had been used by the clothier in whose little shop Slater's new machinery now stood. It was deep winter, and the Blackstone River was frozen over, so that Slater was obliged to crawl down and break up the ice around the wheel. When the wheel turned over, his machinery began to hum.

On December 20, 1790, Samuel Slater's mill produced the first cotton yarn ever made automatically in America. It was strong and of good quality, suitable for sheetings and other types of heavy cotton goods; soon Slater was turning out yarn fine enough to be woven into shirtings, checks, ginghams, and stockings, all of which had until then been imported from Europe. Good cotton cloth woven at home from English yarn had cost from forty to fifty cents per yard, but soon Slater brought the cost down as low as nine cents. For the remainder of that first winter, unable to get anyone else to do the job, Slater spent two or three hours each morning before breakfast breaking the river ice to start the water wheel. Daily it left him soaking wet and numb from exposure; his health was affected for the rest of his life.

The little mill started with four employees, but by the end of one month Slater had nine hands at work, most of them children. In this he was following the practice in England, where entire families were employed in the mills. Early English millowners had found children more agile and dexterous than adults, their quick fingers and small hands tending the moving parts more easily. Slater, like other pioneer millowners dealing with small working forces, was able to maintain a paternalistic attitude toward the young persons in his charge; until the coming of the factory system and absentee ownership, child labor was not the evil it later became. Slater introduced a number of social customs he had learned in the Arkwright and Strutt mills. For his workers he built the first Sunday school in New England and there provided instruction in reading, writing, and arithmetic, as well as in religion. Later he promoted common day schools for his mill hands, often paying the teachers' wages out of his own pocket.

Proudly Slater sent a sample of his yarn back to Strutt in Derbyshire, who pronounced it excellent. Yet Americans hesitated to use it, preferring traditional hand-spun linen yarn or machine-made cotton yarn imported from England. Within four months Moses Brown was writing to the owners of a little factory in Beverly, Massachusetts, run by a relative, proposing a joint petition to Congress: Why not raise the duties on imported cotton goods? Some of the proceeds could be given to southern cotton farmers as a bounty for upgrading their raw cotton, and some could be presented to the infant textile industry as a subsidy.

Next, Brown arranged to transmit to Alexander Hamilton, secretary of the treasury and already known as a supporter of industry, a sample of Slater's yarn and of the first cotton check made from it, along with various suggestions for encouraging the new textile manufactures. He reported to Hamilton that within a year machinery and mills could be erected to supply enough yarn for the entire nation. Two months later, when Hamilton presented to Congress his famous *Report on Manufactures,* he mentioned "the manufactory at Providence [which] has the merit of being the first in introducing into the United States the celebrated cotton mill."

By the end of their first ten months of operations, Almy, Brown & Slater had sold almost 8,000 yards of cloth produced by home weavers from their yarns. After twenty months the factory was turning out more yarn than the weavers in its immediate vicinity could use; a surplus of 2,000 pounds had piled up. Desperately, Moses Brown appealed to Slater, "Thee must shut down thy gates or thee will spin all my farms into cotton yarn."

It was at this point that the full force of Slater's revolutionary processes began to become apparent. To dispose of their surplus the partners began to employ agents in Salem, New York, Baltimore, and Philadelphia, and so encouraging were the sales that it became obvious to them that their potential market was enormous. In 1791, therefore, they closed the little mill and built nearby a more efficient factory designed to accommodate all the processes of yarn manufacturing under one roof. It was opened in 1793. (Now the Old Slater Mill Museum, the building still stands today.)

As of December, 1792, the partners' ledgers had shown a credit in Slater's name of £882, representing his share of the proceeds from the sale of yarn spun by his mill. From then on both he and the infant industry he had helped to create prospered rapidly. The factory was no longer a neighborhood affair but sought its markets in a wider world. When the War of 1812 had ended, there were 165 mills in Rhode Island, Massachusetts, and Connecticut alone, many of them started by former employees of Slater who had gone into business for themselves. By this time Slater, too, had branched out; he owned at least seven mills, either outright or in partnership. An important mill town in Rhode Island already bore the name of Slatersville. Around three new cotton, woolen, and thread mills which he built in Massachusetts, a new textile center sprang up which became the town of Webster. Later, his far-reaching enterprise carried him to Amoskeag Falls on the Merrimac River; in 1822 he bought an interest in a small mill already established there, and in 1826 erected a new mill which became the famous Amoskeag Manufacturing Company, hub of an even greater textile center—Manchester, New Hampshire.

President James Monroe had come to Pawtucket in 1817 to visit the "Old Mill," which was then the largest cotton mill in the nation, containing 5,170 spindles. It had started with 72. Slater himself conducted his distinguished visitor through the factory and proudly showed him his original spinning frame, still running after 27 years. Some years later another President, Andrew Jackson, visited Pawtucket, and when he was told that Slater was confined to his house by rheumatism brought on from that first winter of breaking the ice on the Blackstone, Old Hickory went to pay his respects to the invalid. Courteously addressing Slater as "the Father of American Manufactures," General Jackson said:

"I understand you taught us how to spin, so as to rival Great Britain in her manufactures; you set all these thousands of spindles to work, which I have been delighted in viewing, and which have made so many happy, by a lucrative employment."

Slater thanked his visitor politely and with the dry wit for which he was well known replied:

"Yes, Sir, I suppose that I gave out the psalm, and they have been singing to the tune ever since."

By the time he died in 1835, Slater had become generally recognized as the country's leading textile industrialist. In addition to his cotton and woolen manufactures, he had founded a bank and a textile-machinery

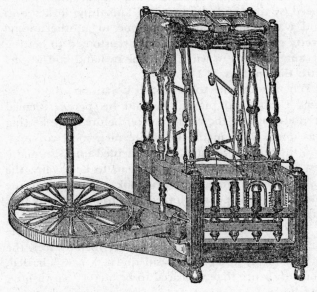

One of the foundations of the English factory system, and a machine with which Slater was familiar, was the Arkwright spinning frame, or throstle frame, invented about 1768.

factory and had helped promote several turnpikes, including a road from Providence to Pawtucket and another from Worcester, Massachusetts, to Norwich, Connecticut. At his death Moses Brown, who survived him, estimated Slater's estate at $1,200,000—a remarkable achievement in those early days of the nineteenth century.

The industry Slater had founded 45 years earlier had shown phenomenal growth by the year he died. In 1790 the estimated value of all American manufactured goods barely exceeded $20,000,000, and the domestic cotton crop was about 2,000,000 pounds. By 1835 cotton manufactured goods alone were valued in excess of $47,000,000, and that single industry was consuming almost 80,000,000 pounds of cotton annually. Few men in our history have lived to see such tremendous economic changes wrought in one lifetime by their own efforts.

The social changes which Samuel Slater witnessed and helped to further were even more far-reaching.

When he arrived in 1789 America was a nation of small farmers and artisans. By the time he died, and to a considerable extent because of his accomplishments, many artisans had become mill hands.

Three years after Slater's mill began operations, a young Yale graduate named Eli Whitney, visiting a Georgia plantation, devised the cotton gin, and this, in combination with English cotton mills and American ones like Slater's in New England, enormously stimulated the cotton economy (and the slave-labor system) of the South. Simultaneously, and paradoxically, Slater and Whitney helped fasten on the North an industrial economy which would defeat the South when the long-standing economic conflict between the two sections flared out at last in civil war.

Arnold Welles is a great-great-grandson of Samuel Slater. Graduated from Yale with honors in American history, he is now in the investment business and divides his time between Savannah, Georgia, and Northeast Harbor, Maine.

The Canny Cayuse CONTINUED FROM PAGE 11

quired, since the horses run out, turn the stake, and come back to the starting point.) The first horse to get home is the winner. No account is made of the start, each rider depending on his shrewdness to get the advantage in this part of the race.

Indians are enthusiastic gamblers, with a certain kind of pride and, to do them justice, honor as well in conducting their races. No disputes, either about the starting or the outcome, ever arise among themselves, and seldom with white men. They take sides with their own people always and bet, when the chances are against them, from pride. The prevailing idea that they are always cool and stoical is not correct. They become very excited at horse races, but not, generally, until the race begins. While the preliminaries are being arranged they are serious, even solemn-looking fellows, and with great dignity come up with the money to bet.

Capable of dissembling, I should think they were, from the cool face of How-lish-wam-po when the money was being counted out by the hundreds in twenty-dollar gold pieces—not a few, but handfuls of twenties. One could not have detected the slightest twinkle in his eye or any other sign that he knew that Joe Crabb had stolen his horse and run him secretly. Cool, calm, earnest as if he were saying mass, this chieftain came up and handed over his money to the stakeholder, while numerous bets were being arranged between the other Indians and white men. Horses were

wagered, tied together, and led away. Many a fellow had brought extras with him for the express purpose of gambling, expecting, of course, to take home twice the number in the evening.

Crabb had confided the secret of his stolen run to a few friends, advising them to place bets and win all the horses they wanted. There was no danger; he knew what he was talking about. He knew the Indian horse's speed by time and also by trial. This thing leaked out, and was communicated from one to another. Some pretty good men who were not accustomed to betting became anxious to win a pony or two and laid wagers with the Indians.

When someone told How-lish-wam-po about the trick Crabb had played, he and his people seemed anxious to have the race come off before more betting was done. This made the white men more anxious, and they urged, boasted, and ridiculed until, in manifest desperation, the Indians began to bet again; the noble white man generously took advantage of the Indian's hot blood and forced him to make many bets that he appeared to shun.

The horses were brought out to start, and while Crabb's imported horse looked every inch a racer, the Indian horse stood with head down, a rough-haired, uncouth brute that appeared to be a cross between ox and horse.

The presence and appearance of the horses was the signal for another charge on the Indians and their few white friends, who, having learned about Crabb's trick from the chief, came in sympathy to the Indians' rescue.

Money, coats, hats, saddles, pistols, pocket knives, cattle, horses, and all kinds of property were staked on the race. The Indians, in their apparent desperation, drove up another band of ponies, and in madness wagered them also.

When the final starting time came, a pure-minded, innocent man would have felt great pity for the poor, dejected-looking Indians at the sight of their faces, now so full of anxiety; and certainly the pinto, on which they had staked so much, did not promise any hope; he stood unconcerned while his competitor was stripped of his blanket, disclosing a nice little jockey saddle and silver-mounted bridle.

His whole bearing indicated his superiority. With his thin nostrils, pointed ears, arched neck, sleek coat, and polished limbs that touched the ground with burnished steel, he disdained to stand still while his gayly dressed rider, in a blue cap, crimson jacket, and white pants tucked into boots embellished with silver-plated spurs, was being mounted. This required two or three experts to assist, so restless was this fine thoroughbred to throw dirt into the eyes of his sleepy-looking rival. The Indian horse stood unmoved, uncovered, without saddle, bridle, or anything save a small hair rope on his lower jaw; his mane and tail were unkempt, his coat rough and ill-looking.

At his right side stood a little Indian boy, with head close shaved and a blanket around him. To all appearances he was unconscious that anything unusual was expected. Meanwhile, the other rider's horse was making furious plunges to get away.

How-lish-wam-po was in no hurry, really; indeed, things were going very much to his satisfaction. He was willing to see the other man's horse chafe and fret —the more the better; and he cared nothing for the sponge that was used to moisten the mouth of the great racer.

Look away down the long line of white men and Indians; and on the low hills above see the crowd eager to witness the first jump!

The chief gives a quiet signal to the Indian boy. The blanket drops from the boy's shoulders, and the yellow-skinned, gaunt-looking sprite bestrides the Indian horse, holding in his left hand the hair rope that is to serve him for a bridle and in his right a small bundle of dried willows.

Presto! The stupid-looking Indian horse is instantly transformed into a beautiful, animated racer. His eyes seem almost human. His ears do not droop now, but by their quick alternate motions give signs of readiness; he stamps his feet, slowly at first, but faster and more impatiently the moment it is intimated that he may go; the other horse is making efforts to escape, his masters maneuvering him for the advantage.

The little Indian boy manages his horse alone as the chief gives quiet signs. Three times they come up to the scratch without a start. Crabb now seems very solicitous about the race. I think, probably, he has by this time found the hornet in his hat; at all events, he is pale, and his rider exhibits signs of uneasiness.

At length, thinking to take what western sportsmen call a "bulge," he says, "Ready!" "Go!" says the little Indian boy, and away go twenty thousand dollars on the heels of the Indian horse, twenty feet in the lead before the other crosses the mark and making the gap wider at every bound.

Away go the flying horses, and several thousand eyes follow the yellow rider, still ahead, as the horses grow smaller and smaller in the distance, until the Indian horse turns the stake at the farther end. Now they come, seeming to increase in size as they approach, the yellow rider still in advance. Crabb gasps for breath and declares that his horse "will yet win."

The eagle eye of the old chief lights up as they come nearer, his rider still leading. The excitement is now beyond description. Look again!—the Indian boy nears the starting point alone, rattling his dry willows over a horse that, considering the nature of the turf, is making the fastest time on record.

The Indians along the line fall in and run beside the victorious racer, encouraging him with wild, unearthly shouts while he crosses the finish line, having run the five and one-fourth miles and eighty-three yards in the unprecedented time of nine minutes and fifty-one seconds, and having won the race and the money, much to the joy of the Indians and their few friends, but to the grief of Crabb and his many friends. He, without waiting to hear from the judges, runs down the track nearly a mile and rushes up to the gayly dressed jockey in his silver spurs, white pants, blue cap, and crimson jacket. He has dismounted and is leading the now-docile, fine-blooded English racer by his silver mountings. Crabb inquires, "What's the matter, Jimmy?"

"Matter? Why, this hoss can't run a bit. That's what's the matter."

Before leaving this subject, it is proper to state that How-lish-wam-po gave back to Crabb the saddle horse he had won from him, and also money to travel on; he added a word of caution about stealing out one's competitor's horse and having a race all alone, remarking dryly, "*Me-si-ka wake cum-tux ic-ta mamook ni-ka tru-i-tan klat-a-wa* [You did not know how to make my horse run]. *Cla-hoy-um* [Good-by], Crabb."

CONTINUED FROM PAGE 14

wheeler, anchored in the same bay to receive the total surrender of the empire that had turned on the republic that had first awakened it from medieval slumber.

Old World nations generally look on diplomacy as a fine art and have been served by generations of professionals schooled in its forms and graces. On the other hand, our own American tradition, reared in isolation, has been to discard that idea and to see in diplomacy something of an alien luxury weighted from time to time with sudden necessity. So we have let ourselves be represented abroad over the generations by a unique amalgam of trained and amateur talent ranging from scholars and eminent sportsmen to deserving meat packers. Of our choices few have been more original than that of the brassbound commodore asked to conduct one of the most demanding and delicate diplomatic negotiations in our history; in terms of results achieved, few choices have been more brilliant.

A fact our schoolbooks sometimes neglect to teach is that Perry's expedition, undertaken by special decision of President and Cabinet, was at bottom an act of aggression and a virtual challenge to war. Perry's genius, for all his bluster and his pivot guns, lay in his preventing an actual war and in achieving a peaceable agreement that surmounted immense barriers of language, culture, suspicion, and ignorance and afforded satisfaction and respect all around. In bringing this about, he was diplomatic enough to know that he must yield on some points—more than the fire-eaters at home liked—in order to persuade the Japanese to yield on others. The question was which points to barter and whose face to save. No one had trained Old Matt Perry to be a diplomat. He came by the art instinctively, by dint of extraordinary human comprehension and native wit—qualities without which even the best-schooled ambassadors fail.

The American Republic had sought to isolate itself from dynastic Europe, only to find itself in 1850 moving out beyond its own continent into the far Pacific. For its part, the Japanese Empire, after some unhappy experiences with European traders and missionaries, had isolated itself in 1825 from virtually the entire outside world. The difference between the two withdrawals was that Japan's remained recessive while America's became aggressive. Under the encrusted shogun who ruled in the emperor's name, Japan virtually declared the nineteenth century out of bounds.

Ships of foreign infidels were prohibited under pain of armed attack from entering Japanese ports, while Japanese subjects were similarly prevented from sailing further from the islands than junks, carefully limited to coastwise size, could carry them. This, thought the shogun, would keep their sacred soil and customs inviolate for all time to come. The Japanese failed to reckon with Yankee whalers, now scouring the nearby seas, or with American merchantmen bound for Canton and anxious for a port of call for business, coaling and provisions, or with the California gold rush, now bringing masses of Americans to the Pacific water's edge, eyes turning toward the Orient.

Moreover, they failed to realize the drive and bumptiousness of these white devils five thousand miles away. While the samurai went through their ancient rituals with silken robes, paper banners, lacquered swords, and weird cardboard headgear, in America such words as these were resounding: "It is our Manifest Destiny to implant ourselves in Asia" (The New York *Herald*); "The apparition of the Caucasian race rising upon the Yellow race . . . must wake up and reanimate the torpid body of Asia. . . . The moral and intellectual superiority of the White race will do the rest" (Senator Thomas Hart Benton); "The 'Gate of the Sun,' as the islanders call their empire, must open voluntarily or perforce. . . . The time has come for it in the providence of God" (*The Presbyterian Review*).

Finally, the old courtiers of Yedo failed to understand one of the first rules of aristocracy—courtesy—and it was this that was to prove their immediate undoing. When shipwrecked American seamen or vessels in distress sought succor on their shores, the Japanese made short shrift of them, jailing whole crews as suspects, interlopers, and spies, thereby giving the American State Department a splendid opportunity to point out that this sort of thing just wouldn't do: the rights of nations also involved elementary human duties, and Commodore Perry was coming to clarify this matter—and to obtain open ports and coaling stations, to boot.

"Invasion of Japan!" trumpeted New York newspapers when Perry's squadron set forth. Meanwhile the *Times* of London, looking down its nose at the presumptuous Yankees, snorted that it wondered "whether the Emperor of Japan would receive Commodore Perry with the most indignation or most contempt." Would the mission to bring American reason to the mysterious "half-barbarians" succeed? There were doubting voices even at home. The Baltimore *Sun* remarked sardonically that Perry would set out "about the same time with Rufus Porter's aerial ship."

With such words whirling about him, it was clear to the commander-diplomat that he must bring home a triumph—if not of one sort, then another.

As one officer who had served under him as far back as Mexican War days remarked, Perry was "a bluff yet dignified man, heavy and not graceful, something of a martinet; a duty man all over, held something in awe by junior officers, and having little to do with them; seriously courteous to others. The ship seemed to have a sense of importance because he was on board." A crewman added, "So long as ye walk a chalk line there couldn't be a fairer man than the Commodore, but God help ye if ye slip off that line!"

Well-born, haughty, meticulously white-gloved and epauletted, sporting magnificently curled eyebrows over his piercing eyes and long, disdainful nose, Perry was the very model of a theatrical admiral—with one difference: he knew precisely how and when to apply his theatrics to the impressionable Japanese. In 1846 a previous American naval visitor to Japan, the undemonstrative Commodore James Biddle in U.S.S. *Columbus,* had suffered a humiliating rebuff when he was struck or pushed by a Nipponese soldier as he descended into a junk alongside his ship. Biddle had done nothing about it save to say that he would be satisfied if the man were handled under the laws of his own land. The Japanese would have been more impressed if Biddle had forthwith drawn his saber and struck the man's head off; they looked upon the visitor and the Navy he represented as craven. Matt Perry wasn't going to have any more of *that.* Yet neither (and this he kept to himself) was he going to lord it over the Nipponese simply because he had the bigger guns. From the side-whiskered Samuel Wells Williams, whom he had taken aboard as America's first orientalist and expert in Far Eastern languages, Perry had learned of the kind of thing that was happening on the China coast as roughshod Western concessionaires and their opium-selling local confederates took over.

A Japanese sketch of Commodore Perry

He wasn't going to have any of *that,* either.

He must be magisterial and grand, he decided (this was not difficult for the Commodore), but he must also be human. Japan appreciated this—although it took the Japanese several generations to fully comprehend it.

America knew little about Japan on the eve of Perry's expedition, and Japan knew even less about America. There had been prior contact of a sort; in fact, over a hundred American ships, curious, had at various times dared the approach to the forbidden islands, but usually they were just driven off. In Japan, though officials tried to squelch even the mention of the sea-borne Yankees, a comparable curiosity had grown as to what Americans were like. Rumors coming from Dutch traders had told of the imminent approach of an American fleet of black ships, and an old ballad went around, very much as had the legends in Montezuma's Mexico of the advent of strange gods under white sails:

> Through a black night of cloud and rain,
>   The Black Ship plies her way,
> An alien thing of evil mien,
>   Across the waters gray.
>
> Down in her hold, there labor men
>   Of jet black visage dread;
> While, fair of face, stand by her guns
>   Grim hundreds clad in red.

So a translation of the ballad by a Japanese scholar runs.

Some more specific information about the Americans was also available. A young Japanese sailor named Nakahama Manjiro, shipwrecked in the Pacific in 1841, had been picked up by an American vessel out of Fairhaven, Massachusetts. Under the simpler name of John Mung, he had been brought to the United States as a curiosity [AMERICAN HERITAGE, December, 1956]. From this experience he had managed to return home and to report that "the people of America are upright and generous, and do no evil. . . . Refined people do not drink intoxicants, and only a small

95

quantity, if they do. Vulgar people drink like the Japanese. . . . Husband and wife are exceedingly affectionate to each other, and the happiness of the home is unparalleled in other countries. The women do not use rouge, powder and the like." But while these discoveries by Japan's first pro-American greatly whetted the curiosity of the younger generation, they were not prepared for what descended on them on July 8, 1853, near the gates of their own imperial capital.

"Popular commotion at the news of 'a foreign invasion' was beyond description," writes a Japanese chronicler. "The whole city was in an uproar. In all directions were seen mothers flying with children in their arms, and men with mothers on their backs. Rumors of an immediate action, exaggerated each time they were communicated from mouth to mouth, added horror to the horror-stricken. The tramp of war-horses, the chatter of armed warriors, the noise of carts, the parade of firemen, the incessant tolling bells, the shrieks of women, the cries of children, dinning all the streets of a city of more than a million souls, made confusion worse confounded."

Down the bay, meanwhile, gesticulating Japanese officials in guard boats converged to try to stop this ruthless violation of their country's laws, while a boatload of artists came alongside the paddle-wheelers to record the scene for posterity. The officials tried to clamber aboard, but, in accordance with Perry's flag-hoist, they were held back with bared steel. The artists did better, lingering in the lee of the black ships to catch glimpses of guns, fantastic machinery, marines, and of a gilded, godlike, white-gloved personage whose lieutenants soon made it known that he was the American Lord of the Forbidden Interior.

An old Japanese manual shows how port officials were indoctrinated to deal with unwanted visitors such as these. They were to say, in case an English-speaking ship hove into sight of land, "Hô deyu do" (How do you do?). Next, they were to say, in pidgin, "We are officer in Yudo, and he is interpreter, tell him what you please." (This, phonetically, came out as *We e-ru ofuhishu-ru in i-doo endo hi isu interupuritoru te-ru himu watto yu-purissu.*") Then, said the manual, they were to challenge the visitors with such remarks as "Is here anybody wich can understand duch or the Rusch language among the maning? . . . From wence come thit ship? . . . At sea of Jappan the foreigner may not fish. . . . You must go way with first speedy wind. . . . It is a great prohibition of Jappan to negotiate with strangers. . . . We have often warnt your country man, that they must no more come here, what is reason of coming you?"

It was with patter such as this that Japanese officials tried to climb aboard, meanwhile—in case the Americans didn't understand pidgin—holding up a scroll written in French ordering the ships to leave. The Lord of the Forbidden Interior, secreting himself in his quarters, produced S. Wells Williams and H. A. L. Portman, who, speaking in Japanese and Dutch, tried to make several things clear. First of all, the American commander would receive no one aboard his flagship but a functionary of the highest rank. As his official narrative puts it, Perry had determined "to meet the Japanese on their own ground, and exhibit toward them a little of their own exclusive policy. If they stood on their dignity and assumed superiority, that was a game at which he could play as well as they."

Furthermore, having read every available book and tract on Japan before setting forth, Perry had been impressed by evidences of Japanese evasiveness, mendacity, and duplicity. So he began by being somewhat mendacious himself. Through the closed door of his cabin he instructed Professor Williams to say that the rank of the American lord whose pennant flew at the foretruck was that of admiral. (The Japanese could not be expected to know that no admiral then existed in the entire American fleet.)

"We have the vice-governor of Uraga aboard," explained an official in a lacquered hat, coming alongside in a barge. "He is of very high rank."

But Perry was not receiving any vice-governors, and as guard boats and the artists edged closer, armed crews manned the rails of his ships. "Why did you not bring the governor?" his interpreter called down.

"He is forbidden to board ships. Will the Lord of the Forbidden Interior designate an officer of rank low enough to talk to the vice-governor?"

Perry, from behind his door, appointed his flag lieutenant. Round one in establishing official relations with the Japanese had been won.

Lieutenant Contee, admitting Vice-Governor Sabe-rosuke on board—the first Japanese emissary to be received on an American ship—began by flatly insisting that "no boats shall hang around our vessels to watch them."

"It is Japanese custom," was the answer.

"We too have our customs, and with men-of-war one of the laws is that no boat is allowed to come within a certain range."

"What is name of thit ship, how many people, guns?"

". . . We are armed ships, and our custom is never to answer such questions."

No one had ever talked like this to the Japanese before. What came next was even more formidable. The lieutenant explained that his commander had brought a letter from the President of the United States to the Emperor of Japan, and that he wished a suitable officer sent on board to receive a copy of it, in order that a day might be fixed for formal delivery of the original. The Vice-Governor, no doubt uneasily aware, as he stood in his silks aboard U.S.S. *Susquehanna,* that his head might come off on his return to shore unless he persuaded the white devils to leave, countered that in any case the American squadron must quit Yedo Bay and proceed down the coast to Nagasaki, the only port where foreign business could be transacted. In reply to this he was told that the American admiral had come here purposely because it was near the capital; that he would not move on to Nagasaki; that he expected the letter to be properly received where he was; that "his intentions were perfectly friendly, but that he would allow no indignity." Moreover, if the guard boats were not removed at once, they would be dispersed by force. The unhappy Saberosuke removed them at once. Round two was won.

At this distance the attitudes Perry struck on that first day in Japan smack of the saber-rattling that was to mark American diplomacy in many outlying seas during the second half of his century. Yet actually his mission cast its shadow even further ahead and looked toward a time of East-West equality and friendship. Everything depended on how Perry read his instructions—which admittedly were perhaps the most sweeping yet tantalizing ones ever given an emissary of the United States.

On one hand President Fillmore's State Department had told him to impress upon the Japanese that the approach of Americans into their area was inevitable and to demand that they abandon their policy of enmity. This was an ultimatum, no less, as the President himself hinted when he described Perry's ships as "persuaders." On the other, the Commodore was warned that his mission was "necessarily of a pacific character" and that he was not to use force except in self-defense. In his contact with the Japanese, "who are said to be proud and vindictive," he was to be at the same time "courteous and conciliatory" and "firm and decided." He was to "submit with patience and forbearance to acts of discourtesy . . . by a people unfamiliar with our ways," yet he was to allow no insult. This, said the directive, placed in his hands "large discretionary powers"—which indeed it did, including the power to destroy himself by a misstep in either direction. Finally, after having virtually washed its hands in advance of any blunders its emissary might commit, Washington bethought itself again and handed him the sop that "any error of judgment" on his part might be viewed with "indulgence"—i.e. he might escape court-martial after all if things went wrong.

Such self-contradictory orders, by the challenge they offer his own inventiveness, can either paralyze an envoy or make him. They made Perry.

His first duty as a commander, of course, was to guard his ships against attack. No coastal batteries had yet fired on him from the surrounding headlands. Yet as he lay at anchor and night approached, the possibility remained that war lords might yet converge in the hills to descend upon him with every weapon at their command. Perry was of a steeled, suspicious nature, yet not more so than the occasion required. For as news of his arrival spread, precisely this sort of surprise attack was being weighed by the shogun's council, which on the appearance of the American squadron had been seized with a panic little less than that of the common people of the capital.

In the days that followed, while the government was floundering over what to do or say, its agents on the spot practiced their own Oriental variety of psychological warfare, sending out to the ships negotiators bearing deceptive instructions, false names and imaginary titles. They went to elaborate lengths to ensure that when Perry was received on shore, he would be conducted only to a makeshift building constructed for the purpose and would not be permitted to defile the sacred premises of official Japan. In this Gilbert and Sullivan masquerade, however, the shogun's men found themselves matched by a comparable American actor whose bluff airs concealed his own extraordinary guile. Perry would, in fact, have made an ideal admiral of Japan.

While inquisitive eyes ran over his ships and their armament, it was explained to Perry that months —many months—would pass before he could expect to receive an answer to the President's letter. Very well, he replied, with a look of infinite patience; he had time and would take his ships to the China coast for the fall and winter and come back for the answer early the following year. Some of his officers dropped the implication that he might then return with an augmented force.

Before leaving to give the rulers time to think, Perry made one splendid appearance at the landing place they had grudgingly prepared for him at Kurihama. On the appointed day, all his ships took station in line offshore to guard against possible treachery. All his officers donned full dress, while bannered Japanese barges hovered about and silken screens bearing the imperial arms were set up on land. Then fifteen U.S. cutters and longboats, bearing officers, pipe-clayed marines, sailors in Sunday blues, and two bands, rowed to the temporary wharf. Captain Franklin Buchanan

TEXT CONTINUED ON PAGE 100

What's Seen and

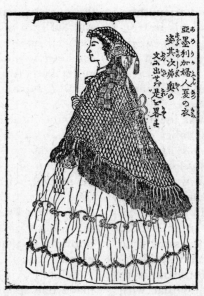

The illustrations on these pages come from an abundantly illustrated, three-volume Japanese tourist guide to Yokohama published in the years after Perry's visit. Then foreigners flocked to the city to open trade, and Japanese flocked from near and far to ogle the foreigners. In the drawings the streets and shops are all carefully identified and the odd garments and odder mannerisms of the foreigners gleefully noted. "American men and women have come from several thousand ri away," says *What's Seen and Heard in Yokohama*, "and from several other countries such as Holland, England, France, Portugal, Russia, and black men from Africa and India. Yokohama is becoming a center of world trade. This is the first time such a thing happens in the history of Japan. These high-ranking foreigners are ones who are important in their own countries and they come from well-known families of

"Foreign seamen being

"American woman's summer attire."

"This game of balls, similar to a played with long sticks to hit the is played on holidays such as Sun-

"Foreigners who went horsebac

Heard in Yokohama

business and they are mild-mannered and courteous. But in regard to the lower class people, there are all kinds of them which is true in any country, but in the practice of commerce there is no one more hard-working than those foreigners. Despite the hardships attendant on the journey the merchants' wives accompanied the husbands so that they could die with their husbands. The deepness of affection is very moving."

The outer pictures on these pages fit together to form two complete views. In order to look at them, Japanese-style, lift both pages and bend them towards each other in the center, fitting the inner edges of the upper left and upper right illustrations together. The early Japanese printers left the entire center section bare and used only one divided illustration per two pages. The pictures from these unique books come from the collection of Harry Shaw Newman of the Old Print Shop.

drunk on Main Street."

ding returning home."

"American woman's winter attire."

children's game in this country is balls from both sides. The game days but not on ordinary days."

of U.S.S. *Susquehanna* jumped ashore from the lead boat, being, as the official chronicle puts it, "the first of the Americans who landed in the kingdom of Japan."

Surrounding the three hundred Americans as they formed into line stood thousands of Japanese warriors in their long, loose vestments, bearing swords, bows, lances, spears, and matchlock guns. Behind them gathered peasants and their womenfolk. Escorted to the newly built reception hall, the American commander and his suite took places on red-covered seats opposite two imperial princes and their retinue, while braziers burned in mid-July amid the suffocating, total silence. Two tall, especially chosen Negro crewmen bore the decorated boxes containing President Fillmore's letter and other documents and placed them before the huddled Japanese—again in utter silence. The princes then bowed and rose, giving the signal to the Commodore to return to his boats and re-embark, "the bands meanwhile playing our national airs with great spirit."

After Perry sailed away, the rulers of Japan were impelled to do something they had never dreamed of before, namely, to ask the advice of their subordinates up and down the country as to how to proceed next. This was the first searing effect of the American visitation, a prophetic interruption in absolute dictatorship. Messengers were rushed out to the feudal chieftains along the length of Honshu, soliciting their opinions. They debated and communed with their ancestors.

Some wanted to fight. One of them, the Prince of Mito, promptly wrote back that there were no less than "ten reasons in favor of war." First, he said, "the annals of our history speak of the exploits of the great, who planted banners on alien soil; but never was the clash of foreign armies heard within the precincts of our holy ground. Let not our generation be the first to see the disgrace of a barbarian army treading on the land where our fathers rest." Secondly, he argued, the Americans might introduce "the evil sect" of Christianity. Furthermore, the Americans might wish to obtain Japanese treasures in exchange for "trashy articles" of trade. Valiant samurai, he added, were assembling to fight the enemy; would it be politic to disappoint them? Moreover, the "haughty demeanor of the barbarians" at their anchorage had provoked the illiterate populace; could the government afford to lag behind? And finally, wasn't this an opportunity to revive flagging Japanese spirits dulled by a too-long peace?

Yet there remained the question of what to fight the barbarians with. Japan had no navy, only weak shore defenses, and there was very little money in the exchequer. "Without warships I feel uneasy with regard to any scheme for pursuing them," argued Lord Ii of Hikone, as well he might. In the end, amid the sputter of conflicting opinions, the shogun's council took the easiest way out—it temporized. Japan, said its decree, was "to evade any definite answer" to the Americans and in effect to play a game of cat and mouse with them. Eventually, it was hoped, the visitors would become discouraged.

The following February the Lord of the Forbidden Interior was back—this time not with four ships but with all of ten, pennants flying, wheels turning, gun muzzles out, crews formed up amidships, and all approaching in faultless alignment. The Japanese had suspected that an armada like this might descend upon them, although they had few inklings of the difficulty Perry had encountered in mustering it on the China coast. They did not know of the barnacled condition of his veteran ships, of the depletion of his crews through disease, desertion, and the end of enlistments, or of his squabbles with the Navy Department to get more ships and men. That winter of waiting, twelve thousand miles removed from Washington, had been a sore test for Commodore and men alike. But morale had revived as the squadron, now raised to the size of a fleet, weighed anchor again in the China Sea. Although Perry's orders were stern, frigates raced each other for first place. "For seven days we kept side by side with the *Macedonian* under shortened sail, the store-ships following with every stick of canvas spread," recounts an officer of U.S.S. *Vandalia*. "At night sometimes advantage was taken by both parties of the darkness to clap on forbidden canvas, and daylight sometimes surprised them before they had it removed."

But off the headlands of Yedo Bay, the Commodore ordered all his ships into line in order to give their second entrance into its glassy waters the precision of a diplomatic march. "The whole bay became filled with black ships," reports a Japanese chronicler. The artists came out in force. Obviously the American Lord was going to have to be given an answer.

This occurred at a viceregal ceremony on March 8, 1854, at Yokohama, from which we may date the opening of regular relations between the two great powers of the Pacific. This time Perry mustered all of 27 boatloads of men supported by three bands, while the Japanese in resignation erected five buildings and assigned the shogun's chief minister to receive him. American marines, their bayonet-tipped rifles at "Present arms!" stood stiffly in a double file as Perry proceeded magisterially to the Treaty House between richly costumed Japanese officials under streamers emblazoned with their own heraldic beasts. At the moment he crossed the threshold, on a signal as precise as it was brilliant, his ships let loose a twenty-one-gun salute in honor of the Emperor, followed by one of seventeen guns for the chief of the high commissioners, while the Japanese ensign was broken out at the masthead of Perry's flagship.

When the smoke had rolled away, the dazzled Japanese were quite in the master showman's hand—or so it seemed. Yes, they said, while His Majesty the Emperor could not of course give satisfactory answers "at once" to all the American proposals, their government was disposed to enter into some friendly arrangement with the United States. In fact (this after some prodding by the Commodore), a treaty of amity might be in order, opening two ports to American commerce as a beginning, and guaranteeing our citizens consular protection.

Then commenced the ceremonial feasting and drinking that was to become the final hazard of Perry's historic expedition. The Japanese began it at the Treaty House by drinking off whole cups of sake bottoms up, explaining to the Americans that it was a Japanese custom for the host to drink first. There was nothing for the Americans to do but follow suit. Soon after came a return engagement on board the American flagship, for which Perry had set aside "live bullocks, some sheep, and a supply of game and poultry." The Japanese swarmed aboard to indulge also in the Commodore's supplies of French wines, champagnes, whiskey, and punch, becoming "quite uproarious" as they proposed healths and toasts (so the official report says) and "shouting at the top of their voices" over the din of the bands and entertainers. Then, when the feast was over, the alcoholized guests astonished their hosts by spreading out long rolls of paper in which they proceeded to wrap up every scrap of food they could lay their hands on, tucking them away into their robes as they entered the longboats. One titled visitor even made off with five saltcellars.

Before this joyous climax there occurred the ceremonial presentation of American gifts for the Emperor and his officials. They included examples of American art and technology, from muskets, swords, clocks, telescopes, farm tools, lifeboats, and a telegraph station to four volumes of Audubon's *Birds of America,* one hundred gallons of Kentucky bourbon, and a miniature locomotive, tender, and passenger car complete with tracks. The Lilliputian train, in particular, was a smash success in a country which had barely entered the horse-and-buggy era; when it was set up near the Treaty House crowds of Japanese screeched with delight every time the American engineer tooted the whistle as he came around the bend. As for the whisky, most of it went straight to the Emperor's palace, where it served further to reduce

effective resistance to the barbarian invaders.

In exchange the Japanese offered the Americans, among other rewards, a special evening performance by prize wrestlers—immense, pot-bellied men encased in rolls of blubber who charged at each other like mastodons, to the mingled delight and amazement of Perry's crews. "All of a sudden they gave a yell and sprang . . . grasping at the armpits, and kept shoving, yelling, tugging, hauling, bawling, twisting and corvetting about, with seemingly no aim whatever," a superior U.S. lieutenant recorded, adding that their style, or lack of it, was something he wasn't accustomed to.

In the end, after such jollifications, Perry got his treaty. It was not as sweeping a one as enthusiasts back home had demanded—in fact, the Japanese recovered in time to surround it with many a reservation—but it did at least open the door of Japan. The hosts hedged on the matter of allowing commercial credit to Americans or of admitting American women at the treaty ports, and on these points Perry yielded, knowing this would all come with time. On the other hand, when the Japanese proposed that American mariners on landing "shall have no intercourse with the Dutch and Chinese," who enjoyed some strictly circumscribed privileges ashore, Perry shot back imperiously, "The Americans will never submit to the restrictions which have been imposed upon the Dutch and Chinese, and any further allusion to such restraints will be considered offensive."

The final upshot was this, as expressed in Article One of the Treaty of Kanagawa [March 31, 1854]: "There shall be a perfect, permanent and universal peace, and a sincere and cordial amity, between the United States of America on the one part, and the Empire of Japan on the other, and between their people, respectively, without exception of persons or places."

As later generations learned to their regret, this article was not always to be observed. But while Perry in opening Japan may also have opened Pandora's box, who could then tell what might someday spring forth from it? The Commodore sailed home, proud, revered even in Japan by literate subjects who had come to think it was high time their country *was* opened up, his holds filled with their gifts and souvenirs, to receive the homage of his fellow citizens as if he had won another war. He had in fact done just that—a war against ignorance and ingrown backwardness—and he had won it without firing a shot.

William Harlan Hale, a contributing editor of The Reporter, *wrote "The Yankee and The Czar" for the February, 1958, issue of* AMERICAN HERITAGE.

General Sherman and the Baltimore

By WALTER LORD

It took a lot of time to run an army, and that was why Major General James B. McPherson, commanding the United States Army of the Tennessee, didn't write his Baltimore fiancee, Emily Hoffman, as often as he should. Not that he loved her any less—he had idolized that unbeatable Victorian combination of blue eyes, golden hair, and chaste daintiness ever since the summer they met just before the war—but he well knew that Emily, the daughter of a prosperous local merchant, was exposed to many attentions, and perhaps he had also heard that a thirty-year-old girl won't wait forever.

In any case, by the summer of 1864 McPherson felt that Emily was growing a little petulant, and, living with that "secesh" family of hers, there was no telling what might happen. Now, with the Atlanta campaign getting under way, there would be even less chance to write, so clearly something had to be done. At this point, McPherson's superior, Lieutenant General William Tecumseh Sherman, took over:

Head-Quarters Military
Division of the Mississippi
Acworth, Ga.
June 9, 1864

My Dear Young Lady,

I hardly feel that I should apologize for intrusion, for I can claim an old acquaintance with your Brother and Sister in California, and feel almost that I know you through them, and others of your honored family. It has come to my knowledge that you are affianced to another close friend and associate of mine Maj Genrl McPherson, and I fear that weighing mighty matters of State but lightly in the Realm of Love, you feel that he gives too much of his time to his Country and too little to you.

His rise in his profession has been rapid steady and well earned. Not a link unbroken. Not a thing omitted. Each step in his progress however has imposed on him fresh duties that as a man and a soldier and still more as a Patriot he could not avoid. I did hope as he returned from Meridian, when his Corps the 17th was entitled to go home on furlough, that he too could steal a month to obey the promptings of his heart, to hasten to Baltimore and I so instructed but by the changes incident to General Grants elevation McPherson succeeded to the Command of a separate Army and Department, and could not leave.

There is no rest for us in this war till you and all can look about you and feel there is Reason & Safety in the Land. God purifies the atmosphere with tempests and storms which fall alike upon the just and unjust, and in like manner he appeases the jarring elements of political discord by wars and famine. Heretofore as a nation we have escaped his wrath, but now with the vehemence of an hundred years accumulation we are in the storm, and would you have us shrink? Would you have us to leave our posts at the Rudder of the Ship in the midst of the Angry Sea of War? What would you think in a California Steamer of the Captain, who regardless of the hundreds of human beings consigned to his Care, would leave his deck, to dally with his loved one below?

But I will not discuss so plain a point with one who bears the honored name of Hoffman, rather tell you of him whose every action I know fills your waking and sleeping thoughts, him so young but so prominent, whose cause is among the gallant and brave, who fight not for oppression and wrong but that the Government bequeathed to us by your an-

Belle

cestors shall not perish in ignominy and insult: but which shall survive in honor & glory, with a power to protect the weak, and shelter the helpless from the terrible disasters of a fratricidal war. I know that at the outset of this war many of the Class with whom you associated, were wont to style us the barbarian hosts of the North, not unlike the hordes that followed Alaric from the wood of northern Europe to desolate the fair field of the dynastic Romans. This may be a parallel but not a fair one. The People of the South were bound to us by a solemn compact which they have broken, and they taunted us with cowardice and poltroonery, which had we borne with submission, we would have passed down to history as a craven and coward race. I doubt even now if our brothers of the South would if free again to choose make so base an issue, but now we go further. We of the North have Rights in the South, in its rivers & vacant Land, the right to come & go when we please, and these Rights as a brave people we cannot & will not surrender on compulsion.

I know McPherson well, as a young man, handsome & noble soldier, activated by motives as pure as those of Washington, and I know that in making my testimony to his high & noble character I will not offend the Girl he loves. Be patient and I know that when the happy day comes for him to stand by your side as one Being identical in heart & human existence you will regard him with a high respect & honor that will convert simple love into something sublime & beautiful.

Yrs with respect   W. T. Sherman

Thus admonished, Emily sat at home trying to be patient while the Union Army swept through Georgia establishing the right "to come & go when we please." By June 22, 1864, General McPherson's forces were probing the outer defenses of Atlanta. But that morning the Confederates launched a surprise counter-attack, and in the confusion McPherson rode forward himself to decide where to deploy his men. As he trotted alone down a country lane, Confederate skirmishers suddenly appeared in the woods not fifty feet away. Someone called on him to surrender, but he merely doffed his cap, wheeled and raced for safety. A fusillade of shots, and McPherson fell from his horse. Within an hour the Union lines were re-established, but the 35-year-old general lay dead in the arms of a broken-hearted Union private.

The following day a messenger appeared at the Baltimore residence of Samuel Hoffman bearing a telegram for Emily's mother. Mrs. Hoffman's only son was in the Confederate service, and that perhaps made it less inexcusable when she remarked, as she handed Emily the message, that here at last was "some good news":

THE AMERICAN TELEGRAPH COMPANY

NEAR ATLANTA JULY 23 1864
REC'D, BALTIMORE, 23 1864,
  TO MRS SAML HOFFMAN   FRANKLIN ST
GENL BARRY DESIRES ME TO SAY THAT GENL MCPHERSON WAS KILLED IN BATTLE YESTERDAY HIS REMAINS WERE SENT TO HIS HOME LAST EVENING IN CHARGE OF HIS STAFF

                   JC VAN DUSEN
                   CAPT & ASST SUPR

Emily fled to her room and locked the door. She was still there three weeks later when a servant handed her a second letter from General Sherman. It was written from outside Atlanta—the city lay under siege now and victory was in sight—but the General's thoughts were far from jubilant:

    HEADQUARTERS, Military Division of the Mississippi
      In the Field, near Atlanta Geo.
            August 5, 1864

Miss Emily Hoffman,
      Baltimore.

My Dear Young Lady,

A letter from your Mother to General Barry on my Staff reminds me that I owe you heartfelt sympathy and a sacred duty of recording the fame of one of our Country's brightest & most glorious Characters. I yield to none on Earth but yourself the right to excel me in lamentations for our Dead Hero. Better the Bride of McPherson dead, than the wife of the richest Merchant of Baltimore.

Why Oh! Why should death's darts reach the young and brilliant instead of older men who could better have been spared. Nothing that I can record will elevate him in your minds memory, but I could tell you many things that would form a bright halo about his image. We were more closely associated than any men in this life. I knew him before you did, when he was a Lieutenant of Engineers in New York we occupied rooms in the same house. Again we met at St. Louis almost at the outset of this unnatural war, and from that day to this we have been closely associated. I see him now, So handsome, so smiling, on his fine black horse, booted & spurred, with his easy seat, the impersonation of the Gallant Knight.

We were at Shiloh together, at Corinth—at Oxford—at Jackson, at Vicksburg, at Meridian, and on this campaign. He had left me but a few minutes to place some of his troops approaching their position, and went through the wood by the same road he had come, and must have encountered the skirmish line of the Rebel Hardee's Corps, which had made a Circuit around the flank of Blair's troops. Though always active and attending in person amidst dangers to his appropriate duties on this occasion he was not exposing himself. He rode over ground he had twice passed that same day, over which hundreds had also passed, by a narrow wood road to the Rear of his Established Line.

He had not been gone from me half an hour before Col. Clark of his Staff rode up to me and reported that McPherson was dead or a prisoner in the hands of the Enemy. He described that he had entered this road but a short distance in the wood some sixty yards ahead of his Staff & orderlies when a loud volley of muskets was heard and in an instant after his fine black horse came out with two wounds, riderless. Very shortly thereafter other members of his staff came to me with his body in an ambulance. We carried it into a house, and laid it on a large table and examined the body. A simple bullet wound high up in the Right breast was all that disfigured his person. All else was as he left me, save his watch & purse were gone.

At this time the Battle was raging hot & fierce quite near

us and lest it should become necessary to burn the house in which we were I directed his personal staff to convey the body to Marietta & thence North to his family. I think he could not have lived three minutes after the fatal shot, and fell from his horse within ten yards of the path or road along which he was riding. I think others will give you more detailed accounts of the attending circumstances. I enclose you a copy of my official letter announcing his death.

The lives of a thousand men such as Davis and Yancey and Toombs and Floyd and Buckner and Greeley and Lovejoy could not atone for that of McPherson. But it is in this world some men by falsehood and agitation raise the storm which falls upon the honorable and young who become involved in its Circles.

Though the cannon booms now, and the angry rattle of musketry tells me that I also will likely pay the same penalty yet while Life lasts I will delight in the Memory of that bright particular star which has gone before to prepare the way for us more hardened sinners who must struggle on to the End.

With affection & respect,
W. T. Sherman

The letter did little good. Emily remained secluded in her room, blinds drawn. Food was left on a tray outside her door, and occasionally she put out a jar of slops. She allowed no one to enter except her sister Dora, who gradually ruined her eyes reading aloud in the gloom. It was exactly a year later—to the very day —when Emily Hoffman finally emerged, to spend the rest of her life in bitter spinsterhood.

Walter Lord, author of A Night to Remember *and* Day of Infamy, *is the grandnephew of the late Miss Hoffman, and now owns the telegram and the two letters from Sherman.*

A Quaker's Letter  To His Watchmaker

"I send thee once more my erroneous watch, which wants thy speedy care and correction. Since the last time he was at thy school, I find, by experience, he is not benefited by thy instruction; thou demandest the fourth of a pound sterling, which thou shalt have, but let thy honest endeavors first earn it. I will board him with thee a little longer, and pay for his table if thou requirest. Let thy whole endeavors and observations be upon him, for he has mightily deviated from the principles of truth; I am afraid he is foul in the inward man—I mean his springs. Prove and try him well with thy adjusting tools of truth, that if possible he may be drawn from the errors of his ways. By the index of his tongue he is a liar, and the motion of his body is ever variable and uncertain. I presume his body is foul, as I have observed; therefore brush him well with thy cleansing instruments from all pollutions, that he may vibrate with regularity and truth; admonish him friendly and with patience, and be not too hasty and rash with thy correction, lest, by endeavoring to reduce him from one error, thou shouldst fling him headlong into another, for he is young and of malleable temper; he may, with due correction, be brought into the path of truth. In fine, let him visit often the motion of the sun, and regulate him by his table of equation; and when thou findest them to agree, send him home with thy bill of moderation, to thy friend Tobias Gowell."

Farm Implements Magazine, 1883, COURTESY OF DAVID B. GREENBERG

F.D.R. vs. the Supreme Court

CONTINUED FROM PAGE 27

official family his stock answer was: "The people are with me; I know it."

Meanwhile a ferment had been working within the court. Some two months before the President had disclosed his plan, the black-robed justices had brooded afresh over the constitutionality of state minimum-wage laws and decided that their previous conclusion in the New York case had been wrong. In a new case the state of Washington, in asking the court to uphold a state minimum-wage law very similar to the New York statute it had invalidated, had directly urged the court to overrule the key precedent on this point, *Adkins* v. *Children's Hospital*, which the timorous New Yorkers had tried merely to circumvent. In December, 1936, the court voted four-to-four to uphold the Washington law and to reverse its own previous decision of only six months before in the New York case.

Four votes were enough to let the challenged statute stand because it had come to the Supreme Court with the sanction of the state of Washington's highest tribunal behind it. Three affirmative votes came from Hughes, Brandeis, and Cardozo. The fourth was that of Justice Roberts, who had switched sides from his position in the New York case, in part at least, because the state of Washington had made a frontal assault on the old precedent, which he felt had been discredited. At the time no one on the court had the slightest inkling of the bill taking shape at the White House, but Hughes was so delighted with Roberts' conversion that he almost hugged him.

Loath to have an issue of such importance disposed of by an even vote, however, Hughes decided to hold this Washington case until Justice Stone returned to the bench. Stone, who was ill, would certainly vote to uphold the state statute. When the Chief Justice revived the issue about February 1, 1937, Stone joined in a complete reversal of the old precedents, but before the opinion could be written and handed down the court found itself under threat of being packed.

Much has been written about this dramatic change of direction by the court, but actually the Washington case did not effect a clean break with the past. The court had upheld broad applications of state powers in both the Blaisdell case (involving the Minnesota Mortgage Moratorium Law) and the Nebbia case (involving the law under which New York was fixing the price of milk). Roberts followed the reasoning of these decisions instead of clinging to the older precedent. His recognition of error indicated that the court did not regard itself as infallible and therefore redounded to its credit.

Support for Roosevelt's judiciary bill further crumbled on April 12, when the court upheld the National Labor Relations Act in the fateful Jones and Laughlin Steel case. The opinion of Chief Justice Hughes was a sweeping confirmation of the power of Congress to regulate industrial relations having a direct impact on interstate commerce. The President claimed credit for the decision but was still not convinced that the court had gone far enough. He turned more heat on wavering legislators on behalf of his bill.

A few weeks later the Senate Judiciary Committee rejected the ill-fated legislation, just before the newly consolidated majority of the court gave its blessing to the Social Security Acts. These events spelled out the Administration's defeat in no uncertain terms, but rear-guard fighting continued because of a strange set of circumstances.

In devising remedies for "the court problem" no one had had the wit or the grace to offer the aged justices a reasonable chance to retire. Even before 1937, both Van Devanter and Sutherland had been eager to lay down their tasks, but Supreme Court justices could cease active service only by resignation, and Congress was then free to reduce their compensation, as indeed it had done in the case of Justice Oliver Wendell Holmes. So the aged judges held on despite some infirmities.

After the court fight began, opponents of the President's bill rushed through Congress a liberalized retirement measure in an effort to forestall a more drastic solution. Senator William E. Borah then persuaded his friend Justice Van Devanter to retire in order to make way for an appointment to the court by Roosevelt, who up to this time had had no opportunity to name a Supreme Court justice. Instead of easing the predicament, however, the sudden creation of a single vacancy threw the White House into near panic.

The President had previously offered the first seat at his disposal to Senator Joseph T. Robinson, a portly and conservative Democratic wheelhorse who, despite grave misgivings as to the judiciary bill's consequences, was directing the fight for it as majority leader of the Senate. If the President should fail to honor his well-known promise to Robinson, he would be left without a friend in the Senate. And fulfillment of the promise would have turned the court fight into a grotesque hoax; for Robinson, at 65, was the antithesis of the "new blood" for which the Roosevelt men were so persistently clamoring. Caught on this horn of his dilemma,

De Groene Amsterdammer

"*How many of them will he get?*"

the President had to continue fighting for his bill as the only means of balancing the prospective Robinson appointment with those of younger and more liberal men.

Thus the fight went on, despite a searing report from the Senate Judiciary Committee. Though it was largely the work of Democratic senators, that report characterized the court bill as "a measure which should be so emphatically rejected that its parallel will never again be presented to the free representatives of the free people of America." At last the Administration sought to compromise, but the Senate had the bit in its teeth. No bill that retained any hint of court-packing was thereafter acceptable.

The unfortunate Joe Robinson was increasingly torn between his distrust of the bill and his ambition to become a justice of the Supreme Court. Outwardly, he fought with desperation against the doom that was closing in on the bill. Secretly, he kept its foes informed about the wavering of senators in his ranks. On July 14, 1937, his sorely troubled heart failed under the strain; his death knell also signaled the end for the judiciary bill. Shortly after Senator Robinson's funeral the Senate formally buried the infamous measure in the usual way—by recommitting it to the Judiciary Committee.

Even this did not bring down the final curtain. F. D. R. struck back by naming as a successor to Justice Van Devanter one of his most ardent supporters in the court fight—a man who would be anathema to his foes in the Senate and who would nevertheless be in a position to command confirmation—Senator Hugo L. Black of Alabama. Regardless of what may be said of Justice Black's subsequent career on the bench, the revenge motive appears to have been a major factor in Roosevelt's nomination of him. If the President found the Senate's discomfiture sweet, however, his satisfaction was short-lived. Shortly after his confirmation, disclosure that Black had once been a member of the Ku Klux Klan brought a fresh public clamor and intensified the bitterness of the whole affair.

Can this strange chapter in our history be regarded as an essential part of the process by which the Constitution has been modernized? Was President Roosevelt right in asserting, long after the fight was over, that he had lost a battle and won a war? Since 1937, undoubtedly, the Supreme Court has in many instances taken a broader view of the powers of Congress than it did before. But this came about without any change in the structure of the court, by an evolutionary process as different from court-packing as is an election from a *coup d'état*.

The chief reason why judicial decisions invalidating acts of Congress began to subside after 1937 was that Congress thereafter exercised greater care in casting its statutes. The reckless draftsmanship of the emergency period was eliminated. Sweeping delegations of power were avoided, and the new regulatory measures were based on the commerce clause instead of on the taxing power. Having fought a terrific battle to save the court from domination by the executive, Congress was especially eager to avoid the type of legislation that might precipitate another showdown.

Some individual judges made changes in their conclusions, as in the minimum-wage cases. But these were less extensive than is generally supposed, and in no instance can they be directly attributed to the court-enlargement plan. Chief Justice Hughes denied emphatically that the court bill had any bearing whatever on any of his decisions, and in no case did he urge his brethren to shade their views to save the court. The "switch-in-time-saves-nine" myth was never anything more than a journalistic wisecrack.

More important than anything else in the evolution of constitutional doctrine since 1937 has been the changed personnel of the Supreme Court. Before F. D. R.'s death in 1945 he had named seven of the nine members of the court and had elevated Stone to the chief justiceship. Though the new justices became involved in turbulent controversies among themselves, they went much further than the Hughes court had done in amplifying the commerce clause and other federal powers. In general the country has accepted and welcomed these new interpretations. But what would have been its attitude and what would now be the standing of the court before the bar of public opinion if its membership had been expanded to fifteen in order to bring about decisions favored by the White House?

If Roosevelt had sponsored a reasonable retirement bill for members of the Supreme Court in 1937, the evolutionary process would have been hastened and this entire sorry chapter in our history could have been avoided. The chief difficulty seems to have been that after his triumphal re-election in 1936 the President was riding too high to deal with the court with the moderation and restraint that should guide the relations of one co-ordinate branch of government to another. He chose a method which might indeed have lifted restraints from Congress and the Administration—there was never much doubt about that—but it would also have imperiled our constitutional system, the central genius of which is its system of checks and balances.

The justices who piloted the court through this difficult period won a double victory. The net effect of the 1935–37 ferment over constitutional issues was to confirm their insistence that judges must take into account changed social and economic conditions as well as past legal precedents. After Justice Roberts

abandoned his four conservative colleagues in the Washington minimum-wage case, they did not again control the court on any vital issue. The views that prevailed were those of Chief Justice Hughes, and of Justices Brandeis, Stone, Cardozo, and Roberts.

The principle for which they struggled was continued independent judgment on the part of the court. They insisted that it must be free to upset an NRA which slopped over the line of constitutional power as well as to uphold an NLRB which did not. With these men still on the bench, the NRA would have gone down in 1938 as readily as it did in 1935. They stood for a Constitution which marched forward—but not to tunes called by the White House or by a spate of new justices suddenly appointed for that purpose.

Contrary to Roosevelt's boast, it was these men who won both the "battle" and the "war" in 1937. Twenty years after the notorious court-enlargement bill went down to defeat, it has scarcely a defender. If it may be credited with having written a salutary lesson in our history, it is only because cooler heads than those of its authors found sage and legitimate means of destroying it. The bill remains one of the major errors of American statesmanship in the current century.

Merlo J. Pusey, associate editor of The Washington Post, *is the author of* The Supreme Court *and of the authorized biography of Charles Evans Hughes, for which he received both the Pulitzer Prize and the Bancroft Prize in 1952.*

The Submarine That Wouldn't Come Up CONTINUED FROM PAGE 51

a long pole extending from its bow. It was called the *David*, and the projection off its bow was a spar torpedo—a pole capable of being raised or lowered from the boat, with a torpedo fitted into a socket at the end of it. It was operated by a crew of four men.

On the night of October 5, the *David*, under command of Lieutenant William T. Glassell, steamed out to the *New Ironsides*, rammed her with the torpedo, and damaged her so badly that she was out of action for the remainder of the siege of Charleston. The explosion poured water down the *David*'s little smokestack and drowned her boiler, and sailors on the ironclad were peppering her with shot; Glassell gave the order to abandon ship. He and James Sullivan, the fireman, were captured in the water, but Engineer James H. Tomb after a while noted that the *David* was drifting away from the ironclad. Returning to the boat, he found Pilot J. Walker Cannon, who could not swim, hanging to it, and the two re-entered it, got the engine going, and brought it back into port.

This was another first, the first time a warship had been damaged by a torpedo boat, and at Charleston enthusiasm reached fever pitch. In this atmosphere, Lieutenant Payne had no difficulty in finding a second crew for the *Hunley*. So the *Hunley* was raised, repairs were made, and the practice runs were resumed. And history repeated itself, this time alongside the wharf at ruined Fort Sumter. The little boat swamped again, and only Payne and two others of the crew escaped. (It might be well to note at this point that no exact count of the men lost on the *Hunley* is ever likely to be made. Her unhappy fame resulted in such garbled reports, even from those close to her, that scarcely two stories agree. All that can be done at this date is to make an informed guess, and on that basis fourteen men had now lost their lives on the submarine.)

For all his enthusiasm, Beauregard began to wonder if the *Hunley* was worth the effort. But at that time, Horace Hunley himself arrived from Mobile with a volunteer crew and a burning conviction that the navy crews simply did not understand how to operate his boat. He asked permission to operate her himself, with a crew who had learned her eccentricities at Mobile.

With some misgivings, Beauregard agreed. The Mobile crew took out the *Hunley*, dived successfully, and returned safely. The general relaxed. Then, on the rainy morning of October 15, in the presence of a large number of persons, Hunley took his boat into the water, submerged, and failed to come up.

The word reached Mobile, and the two young engineers, Dixon and Alexander, who had been assigned to help build the boat, heard it with mixed emotions. Both men were determined now to offer their services for yet another try at operating the *Hunley*. They applied for permission to make the effort, and Beauregard, reserving judgment until the *Hunley* should be raised again, ordered them to report to his chief of staff, General Thomas Jordan.

Beauregard himself was present when the submarine was brought up, and the sight of its interior left an indelible impression on his mind. Fourteen years later he still remembered the horror of it. "The spectacle," he recalled, "was indescribably ghastly; the unfortunate men were contorted into all kinds of horrible attitudes; some clutching candles, evidently endeavoring to force open the manholes; others lying in the bottom tightly grappled together, and the blackened faces of all presented the expression of their despair and agony."

Sickened, he called a halt to the experiments. But Dixon and Alexander pleaded eloquently for a chance to bring some good out of the repeated tragedies. Beauregard hesitated, and General Jordan offered a suggestion: instead of using the *Hunley* as a submarine, why not use it as a *David*? In short, fit it with a spar torpedo instead of the dangerous trailing explosive, and let it attack from the surface.

Under these terms the General consented, or such was his recollection in 1878. But later his resolve may have softened, or the terms were interpreted broadly, for while the *Hunley* acquired a spar torpedo it continued to operate under water.

Meanwhile, Dixon and Alexander were making their own expert appraisal of the story as they pieced it together after the *Hunley* was raised.

The boat had been found on the bottom of the river at an angle of about 35 degrees, her bow deeply buried in the mud. The bolts holding down each hatch cover had been removed, but the hatches were closed. Considerable air and gas escaped when they were lifted. Hunley's body was found forward, his head in the hatchway and his right hand still extended in the dying effort to open the cover. The candle in his hand, significantly, had never been lighted. The sea cock on the forward ballast tank was wide open and the cock wrench lay on the bottom of the boat. In the after hatchway the corpse of Thomas Parks, second-in-command and a member of the firm at whose shop the boat had been built, still pushed at the hatch cover; the sea cock on his tank was closed. Hunley and Parks had died of asphyxiation while the others drowned below them. The clumsy arrangement for dropping the iron keel ballast had failed; the bolts had been partly turned, but not enough to release it.

Studying the grim evidence, the two engineers thought they could agree without question on what had happened. The decisive moment had come immediately after the boat submerged. Hunley had turned the fins to go down and then decided he needed more ballast—that is, more water in his tank to assist in the dive. Without pausing even to light his candle, he had opened the cock. Instantly, the boat dropped so low that the glass panes in the coamings were covered and the craft was plunged in darkness. Hunley began trying to light his candle, the water continued to rush into the tank through the open sea cock, and the boat sank rapidly. The ballast tanks, it will be recalled, were "unfortunately left open on top." Now, Hunley's tank flooded in the darkness.

"The first intimation they would have had of anything being wrong," Alexander wrote in later years, "was the water rising fast, but noiselessly, about their feet in the bottom of the boat. They tried to release the iron keel ballast, but did not turn the keys quite far enough, therefore failed."

The boat was refitted, and Dixon and Alexander went to General Jordan to ask for a crew. Jordan relayed their request to Beauregard, who balked at first but finally agreed to let the Alabamians go aboard the *Indian Chief*, the Confederate Navy's receiving ship, and ask for volunteers. He insisted, however, that they give a full account of the *Hunley*'s past misadventures. This was done, and eventually a crew of volunteer sailors took their places, under command of two lieutenants from an infantry regiment, in a privately owned submarine operated on orders of an army general.

The *Hunley* was off and, if not running, at least limping again.

The attitude of Confederate Navy officers on the scene appears to have been skeptical if not downright hostile. Flag Officer Tucker, asked to provide the submarine with a tow down the harbor, assigned the *David* to the task, with Lieutenant Tomb, one of the heroes of the *New Ironsides* attack, in command. Tomb was directed to report his opinions as to the *Hunley*'s safety and efficiency to Tucker.

Tomb was skeptical, but in the days that followed,

Dixon, Alexander, and their crew appeared to have broken the *Hunley* jinx at last. They made a series of successful dives in Charleston's immediate vicinity, and it was decided the *Hunley* must seek a victim among the blockading vessels outside the bar instead of going out after a monitor, as had been earlier planned. For, alarmed by the success of the *David* in disabling his finest warship, Admiral Dahlgren had ordered chain booms to be placed around the monitors —the *Weehawken,* the *Passaic,* the *Montauk,* the *Catskill,* and the *Nahant.* Accordingly, Dixon was ordered to moor his boat off Battery Marshall on Sullivan's Island, where it could proceed by interior channels to the area where Dahlgren's wooden boats lay.

By now it was November. Quarters for the crew

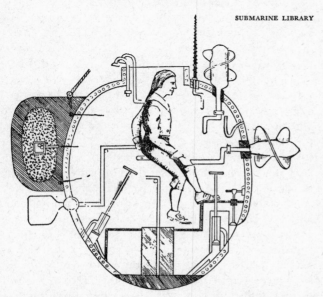

The first true submarine, the Turtle, *invented by patriot David Bushnell in 1776, had a one-man crew and an early-model snorkel. It tried to sink a British fleet off New York.*

were provided at Mount Pleasant, seven miles from the battery, and practice runs were begun in earnest.

A major problem soon became apparent, the matter of distance. The station of the nearest frigate, which they understood was the *Wabash,* was twelve miles away. The *Hunley* could reach a speed of about four miles an hour in comparatively smooth water and light current, but in rough water her speed was much slower. The ideal attack plan, Dixon and Alexander agreed, would be to go out with the ebb tide on a dark, calm night, strike, and come in with the flood tide.

But whole weeks went by, and the wind held contrary. The *Wabash,* or whatever vessel it was that lay off in the distance, was too far for the crew of the *Hunley* to reach by a reasonably safe hour. They ventured out five, six, even seven miles, but each time they were forced to turn back, the men cranking with all their might to avoid drifting out to sea.

In all this time, the *Hunley* showed only one structural fault. The air box, which was supposed to provide fresh air through a pipe while the *Hunley* lay just below the surface, had not worked out well. When ventilation was needed it was necessary to come up high enough for the after-hatch cover to be opened. Several times, when they did this, they could hear conversation and song from Federal picket boats, and they realized how vitally important it was to choose dark nights for their expeditions.

The whole matter of the limited air supply at last led Dixon and his English associate to undertake an experiment. Painfully conscious of their exposed condition and low speed when they had to surface, they decided to find out just how long it was humanly possible for them to stay down without coming up for air.

The Back Bay off Battery Marshall was chosen for the test. All hands agreed they would go out, submerge, sink, and lie on the bottom for as long as possible. When any man felt he had reached the limit of his endurance and must go up for air, he was simply to say, "Up." Regardless of who spoke the word, it was to be considered an order for all hands to obey instantly.

Late one afternoon, after making several brief dives, they were ready. While a crowd of soldiers watched from the bank, unaware of the plan, Dixon and Alexander compared watches, noted the time, and took the *Hunley* down. She sank to the bottom of the bay, the men quit turning the propeller, and the experiment was on.

For a long time they sat motionless, looking silently at one another across the shadows cast by Dixon's candle. Twenty-five minutes passed. The candle went out and could not be relit. Still no one spoke the word that would terminate the experiment.

As the *Hunley* continued to lie on the bottom of the bay, the curiosity of the watching soldiers ashore turned to alarm, and then to a conviction of disaster. A message was sent to General Beauregard, reporting that the ill-fated "coffin" had claimed another crew. Powerless to attempt a rescue, the watchers gradually drifted away as the sun set.

And now, in the darkened boat, the limit was reached at last. A man gasped, *"Up!"* and, in the instant he spoke, every other man aboard echoed the word.

"Start the pumps!"

The bow of the *Hunley* began slowly to rise, but the stern clung to the bottom. Something had gone wrong with Alexander's pump; it was not emptying its tank. As the boat began to tilt dangerously, Alexander made a desperate guess. The valve must be fouled. Working frantically, he felt for the cap of the pump, took it off, lifted the valve, and fumbled for an obstruction.

Seaweed lay thick around the valve. The Englishman snatched it off, replaced the cap, and renewed his pumping. One of the crew had begun to babble incoherently as the stern of the *Hunley* slowly began to rise.

But the worst was over. They reached the surface, and with all the strength he had left Alexander flung open his hatch cover. For a while they slumped, gasping. Then they made for shore. A match was struck, and watches were examined. It had been two hours and thirty-five minutes since the submarine had dived.

Meanwhile, the secret of the *Hunley* had reached the ears of the distracted Admiral Dahlgren. A Confederate deserter gave him a remarkably accurate account of the submarine, her construction, her weaknesses, and her potentialities. Dahlgren had called for precautions against torpedo boats after the *New Ironsides* was attacked, but now he made his orders doubly detailed.

"The ironclads," he directed, "must have their fenders rigged out and their own boats in motion about them. A netting must also be dropped overboard from the ends of the fenders, kept down with shot, and extending along the whole length of the sides, howitzers loaded with canister on the decks and a calcium [light] for each monitor. The tugs and picket boats must be incessantly upon the lookout, when the water is not rough, whether the weather be clear or rainy."

But, as Dahlgren went out nightly to see for himself whether his monitors were maintaining a proper vigil, the "diving torpedo" he feared was watching its opportunity to go against a wooden vessel outside the bar. It was an eventuality the harassed admiral had not considered.

Now that the underwater test had been successful, the *Hunley* resumed her regular schedule, going out as often as the weather permitted and taking even more risks than before in her efforts to reach a target. But still the wind was against her.

About the end of January, 1864, there came an even bigger disappointment. Alexander was ordered back to Mobile to build a breech-loading repeating gun. Alexander departed, crushed, and Dixon set out dejectedly to train a new second-in-command.

So matters stood when, on the night of February 17, the wind turned to fair and the sea grew calm. Dixon decided that, in spite of a bright moon, he could wait no longer. At Battery Marshall, a signal was agreed on for his use in case the *Hunley* wanted a light as a guide for her return trip. The crew filed aboard, the hatches were closed, and the *Hunley* slipped under the water. The time had come at last.

Acting Master Crosby's prompt alarm at sight of the supposed plank floating in the water abeam of the *Housatonic* brought the sloop's captain, officers, and men piling onto the deck. By now a moving phosphorescent light clearly marked the path of the strange object below them.

It had changed direction. At the sound of the call to quarters it had come almost to a halt and then begun to move toward the stern of the vessel. When Captain Charles W. Pickering arrived on deck, the object was already on the *Housatonic*'s starboard quarter.

The sloop, a screw steamer of 1,240 tons launched at Boston late in 1861, carried thirteen guns, but by now it was impossible to use these weapons. The shadow in the water was so near that attempts to train a gun on it were futile. Captain Pickering and several others on deck began firing with revolvers and rifles.

The chain had been slipped, and now the engines began backing. At the time the order was given it was the right thing to do, for the submarine was abeam. But now it was approaching from the starboard quarter, and the *Housatonic*'s engines sent the sloop closer toward its enemy.

It was too late to change direction. Before the men on deck had grasped what was happening, the vessel was shaken by a great explosion between the mainmast and mizzenmast. Timbers and splinters flew through the air; men fell stunned or injured to the deck; the entire stern of the vessel seemed to disintegrate. There was a great rushing of water, an immense cloud of black smoke rose from the stack, and the *Housatonic* went down almost immediately. Less than an hour after Acting Master Crosby had first sighted the mysterious shape in the water, the survivors of the *Housatonic* were being rescued. At muster next morning, only five members of the crew failed to answer.

History had witnessed the first sinking of a warship by a submarine. The feat would not be duplicated for half a century.

A Federal court of inquiry convened aboard the *Wabash* the following week, reviewed the evidence, and found no indication that anyone aboard the sunken ship had been remiss in his duties. Admiral Dahlgren hastened back from Port Royal, redoubled his precautions against torpedo attacks, and called on the Navy Department to offer a large reward to any crew that captured or destroyed a torpedo boat. And in Charleston and Mobile friends of the *Hunley* and her crew waited word of the submarine's fate.

The word did not come for a long time. Not until a Federal picket boat was captured off Fort Sumter did

Beauregard, and the whole Confederacy as well, learn the magnitude of the little submarine's accomplishment. Coupled with this news was the report that Dixon and his men had not been captured, a grim indication that they must have been lost.

It was April before a letter was sent to General Maury, still pressing from Mobile for official word of the *Hunley*'s fate. Captain M. M. Gray, torpedo officer in the Office of Submarine Defenses, expressed the opinion that she had sunk with the *Housatonic*. Gray believed the submarine had gone into the hole made in the *Housatonic* by the explosion and had been unable to muster sufficient power to back out.

It was as good a guess as any. Alexander speculated later that it must have happened just that way. Dixon, he reasoned—in a long memoir in the New Orleans *Picayune* of June 29, 1902, which is the richest source of information about the *Hunley*—had deliberately risked the moonlight in his ardor to sink the sloop, and had been observed by the lookout when he came

to the surface for a final observation before striking her. Not knowing the *Housatonic* was about to back down upon him, he had submerged a few feet and steered for the stern. The combined momentums of the two vessels brought them together sooner and with greater force than he had anticipated, and he and his crew had been unable to back their boat out of disaster.

Partly because of the Federals' justified fear of torpedoes, Charleston did not fall until February 17, 1865. When divers first went down to look at the wreck of the *Housatonic*, they saw no trace of the *Hunley*. But years later she was found, lying on the bottom of the harbor, still pointing toward the vessel she had sunk. Within her still lay the remains of the last crew of the Peripatetic Coffin.

Lydel Sims is a feature writer on the Memphis Commercial Appeal. *He has collaborated on a new book about World War II submarine operations, soon to be published by Little, Brown under the title* War Fish.

The Elusive Swamp Fox CONTINUED FROM PAGE 47

own fort at Nelson's Ferry. Marion dashed to Georgetown and this time took it. Greene himself unsuccessfully laid siege to Ninety-Six, but the enemy soon evacuated it and pulled back and consolidated at Orangeburg on the Edisto. Marion, Sumter, and Lee spent a vigorous summer striking behind the enemy army, ranging almost to Charleston, while Greene refreshed his hard-marched army in the cool oak-and-hickory woods of the High Hills of Santee below Camden.

Late in August Greene came down from the High Hills to fight his last pitched battle of the war, at Eutaw Springs near Nelson's Ferry, on September 8. For the first time since the assault on Savannah in 1779, Marion found himself in formal battle, in command of the right wing of Greene's front line. The whole first line was made up of North and South Carolina militia. It must have seemed strange to Marion's partisans to be there. But for once militia did not panic; before falling back under enemy pressure they delivered seventeen rounds and wrung from Greene praise for a firmness that he said "would have graced the veterans of the great King of Prussia."

It was pretty much a drawn battle. Both sides retreated. But Greene had damaged the British so severely that soon they withdrew into their lines at Charleston and never emerged again.

Though Whigs and Tories murdered each other with unrelenting bitterness for more than a year longer, and hard-hitting raids took men slashing and

shooting through the swamplands, and Marion added more names to his roster of fights, the question of ultimate victory in the South was settled. On the day following the battle of Eutaw Springs, a French fleet returned to Chesapeake Bay in Virginia and sealed the fate of the ambitious English earl whom Greene had driven into a faraway trap at a village called Yorktown.

In December of the next year, 1782, under the gnarled live oaks at Wadboo plantation, Marion discharged his brigade, its mission accomplished.

Today many of Marion's battle sites are under manmade lakes, sacrificed to the need for water power. Others are long lost under towns and roads and domesticated fields, and others simply cannot be identified. But the old maps show where he rode and the brittle documents tell what he did, and it was a magnificent performance.

After the war Marion married his cousin and lived out his last years in comfort as a small planter on the Santee. When he died in 1795, it made scarcely a stir; he was simply another old officer of the Revolution. So, perhaps, it was justice, after all, that Parson Weems came along.

George F. Scheer of Chapel Hill, North Carolina, is now at work on a biography of Marion. He contributed "The Sergeant Major's Strange Mission" to the October, 1957, issue of AMERICAN HERITAGE.

The old-fashioned epitaph, a literary form all its own, runs to both conscious and unconscious humor, as this little sampling bears lasting witness.
The inscriptions come from a number of sources, but we acknowledge the
special help of Peter Beilenson of the Peter Pauper Press in collecting them.

IN
MEMORY OF
LIDIA
WIFE OF
SIMEON PALMER

IN
MEMORY OF
ELIZABETH
WHO SHOULD
HAVE BEEN THE
WIFE OF
SIMEON PALMER
Little Compton, Rhode Island

HERE LIES JOHN COIL
A SON OF TOIL
WHO DIED ON ARIZONA SOIL
HE WAS A MAN OF CONSIDERABLE VIM
BUT THIS HERE AIR WAS TOO HOT FOR HIM
Phoenix, Arizona

WE CAN BUT MOURN OUR LOSS
THOUGH WRETCHED WAS HIS LIFE
DEATH TOOK HIM FROM THE CROSS
ERECTED BY HIS WIFE
Kittery, Maine

HERE LIES THE BODY OF JOHN MOUND
LOST AT SEA AND NEVER FOUND
Winslow, Maine

UNDER THE SOD, UNDER THE TREES
LIES THE BODY OF JONATHAN PEASE
HE IS NOT HERE
BUT ONLY HIS POD:
HE SHELLED OUT HIS PEAS
AND WENT TO HIS GOD
Nantucket, Massachusetts

TO THE MEMORY OF
ABRAHAM BEAULIEU
ACCIDENTLY SHOT APRIL 1844:
AS A MARK OF AFFECTION
FROM HIS BROTHER
Kittery, Maine

SHE LIVED WITH HER HUSBAND
FIFTY YEARS
AND DIED IN THE CONFIDENT HOPE
OF A BETTER LIFE
Burlington, Vermont

HE CALLED
BILL SMITH
A LIAR
Tombstone, Arizona

IN MEMORY OF
ELLEN SHANNON
WHO WAS FATALLY BURNED
BY THE
EXPLOSION OF A LAMP
FILLED WITH
DANFORTH'S NON-EXPLOSIVE
BURNING FLUID
Girard, Pennsylvania

STRANGER CALL THIS NOT
A PLACE OF GLOOM:
TO ME IT IS A PLEASANT SPOT
MY HUSBAND'S TOMB
Bismarck, N. D.